the Lessons

of the

Church Year

Gordon Lathrop

EASTER

PROCLAMATION 6 | SERIES A

FORTRESS PRESS | MINNEAPOLIS

PROCLAMATION 6
Interpreting the Lessons of the Church Year
Series A, Easter

Scripture quotations, unless otherwise noted or translated from the Greek by the author, are from the New Revised Standard Version Bible, copyright © 1989 by the Division of Christian Education of the National Council of Churches in the U.S.A. and used by permission.

Cover design: Ellen Maly
Text design: David Lott

The Library of Congress has cataloged the first four volumes as follows:

Proclamation 6, Series A : interpreting the lessons of the church
year.
  p. cm.
  Contents: [1] Advent/Christmas / J. Christian Beker — [2]
Epiphany / Susan K. Hedahl — [3] Lent / Peter J. Gomes —[4] Holy
Week / Robin Scroggs.
  ISBN 0-8006-4207-4 (v. 1 : alk. paper) — ISBN 0-8006-4208-2 (v.
2 : alk. paper) — ISBN 0-8006-4209-0 (v. 3 : alk. paper) — ISBN 0-8006-4210-4
(v. 4 : alk. paper).
  1. Bible—Homiletical use. 2. Bible—liturgical lessons,
English.
BS534.5P74 1995
251—dc20   95-4622
                      CIP
    Easter / Gordon Lathrop—ISBN 0-8006-4211-2 (v. 5: alk. paper)
    Pentecost 1 / K. C. Hanson—ISBN 0-8006-4212-0 (v. 6: alk. paper)
    Pentecost 2 / Clarice J. Martin—ISBN 0-8006-4213-9 (v. 7: alk. paper)
    Pentecost 3 / William Klassen—ISBN 0-8006-4214-7 (v. 8: alk. paper)

Manufactured in the U.S.A.   AF 1-4211
00 99 98 97 96 1 2 3 4 5 6 7 8 9 10

Contents

In Memoriam

Wyliss M. Starbird

Walter A. Ramshaw

Introduction

Easter is fifty days long: a *pentecost* of days; a week of weeks, plus a day; eight Sundays, eight returns of the day that ancient Christians called the "eighth day."

Easter has been fifty days long since at least the second century. The observance of these days has been intended as an excessive festival to say a word of life beyond all imagining, an intense festival annually to anchor the Christian imagination and the Christian identity. Knowing something about this original meaning of the observance will give to preachers and worship planners a key for understanding the lectionary of the season. Understanding both the festival and the lectionary may help revivify the company of us preachers to do the preaching part of the communal Easter celebration.

A beginning of such understanding is found in this: What Sunday is to the week the fifty days of Easter are to the year. Every Sunday is thus a day for assembly around the risen Lord, and the texts for Sunday are best understood when they are read with that purpose in mind. The fifty days also, as if they were together one single, long day, are a time for such assembly, a great "Lord's day." The texts for these fifty days are then a proclamation of the resurrection in which to anchor the whole year.

So, every Sunday is the eighth day, beginning and ending the seven-day-round of our weekly experience in a communal encounter with something that our weeks could never give us, yet something that, by God's grace and mercy, *is* given here and now. Every Sunday assembly is to be a foretaste of God's great coming day of justice and consolation. The "Lord's day" already foreshadows the "day of the Lord." But then the fifty days, together making up about one-seventh of the year, as if they were the first day in a week of such days, have the same function for the year. In the Christian gatherings during the fifty days, just as in the gathering on the week's first day, we encounter a word that no amount of our days or weeks or years could create. We encounter the word and truth of Jesus' resurrection. We encounter, as the beginning and end of every unit of time, all the mercy that God has worked in the passion, death, resurrection, and promised coming of Christ. This is a word that is in our time from beyond our time, from the end of our times. Thus, the days of such eschatological celebration form a kind of eighth day to the year.

Sunday, the Lord's day, is about the resurrection; it is the weekly communal encounter with the risen one. The biblical texts, read and preached next to the celebration of the Lord's Supper, are one principal means of that encounter. The fifty days, like one single great day, are an annual immersion in the same reality. Although "Every Sunday is a little Easter" is a commonly stated truism, it may be better to assert that "The fifty days are a Sunday to the year." The lectionary we will consider here gives us the texts for that "annual Sunday."

EASTERTIDE: THE EARLIEST MEANING OF THE GREAT FIFTY DAYS

Evidence for the Christian observance of the fifty days as a *laetissimum spatium*, a "most joyful space," is found almost as early as evidence for the observance of Easter—or *pascha*—itself. The Christianization of the passover feast seems to have happened first in mid-second century Asia Minor. There communities observed a Christian version of the "night of vigil for the Lord" (Exod. 12:42), holding it—exactly like the Jews—at the full moon in the first spring month. The Christianized *pascha* then spread throughout the churches and eventually was celebrated on the *Sunday* following the spring full moon, thus becoming, by at least the third century, the annual Sunday feast that we have inherited.

In the late second and early third century, we have evidence from Gaul and from North Africa, as well as from Asia Minor, that this Christian *pascha* inaugurated a fifty-day period of celebration. The communities of Asia Minor that first kept the Christian *pascha* may already have counted fifty days from this feast (Lev. 23:15-16) to their own feast of weeks, keeping the *pentecost* of days as an extension of their Passover. In any case, by the turn of the second to the third century in Africa, Tertullian (ca. 160 – ca. 220), using the convention of the *spring* month as the first month of the year, wrote:

> If there is a new creation in Christ, our solemnities too will be bound to be new: else, if the apostle has erased all devotion absolutely "of seasons, and days, and months, and years," why do we celebrate the passover by an annual rotation in the first month? Why in the fifty ensuing days do we spend our time in all exultation? (*On Fasting*, 14; *Ante-Nicene Fathers* 4:112)

From this passage and many others, we know that in antiquity the fifty-day-long feast, *pascha* and *pentecost* together, arose as a widespread practice far before the emergence of other Christian festivals and second only to Sunday itself.

The earliest Christian *pascha* took from Judaism the custom of gathering in the night and reading the great stories of the saving acts of God for Israel—the exodus story, of course, but also the creation, the flood, the sparing of Isaac, the deliverance of Jonah and of the children in the furnace, and more. But Christians centered these stories around the story of Christ as the saving Lamb, in the account of his death at Passover-time as the great final deliverance of God.

The earliest Christian *pentecost*, then, seems to have taken over the period of the old Jewish "counting of the omer," the calculation of the fifty days from Passover until the spring harvest festival called *shavuoth* ("weeks") and, later, called *pentecost* (applying the Greek name, in this case, to the last day of the fifty-day period). But Christians took the ancient command to rejoice over the liberation of the people from bondage (Deut. 16:9-12) to apply to the entire period, not only to its last day. For them the exultation was because this very period had been the time of the primitive Christian encounter with the risen one who is the ground of all liberation. When *pascha* was moved to Sunday (or, rather, to the night between Saturday to Sunday), the fifty days followed, making them stretch over eight Sundays. Even then, however, the night of *pascha* was primarily an encounter with the story of the cross while the fifty days were an occasion for the stories of the resurrection.

In the ancient church the fifty days were a time for praise and song, for *standing* in prayer—never kneeling—for proclaiming the resurrection and hoping for Christ's coming, for baptizing and for the teaching attendant on baptism. So Tertullian again wrote:

> The passover [*pascha*] affords a more than usually solemn day for baptism; when, withal, the Lord's passion, in which we are baptized, was completed. ... After that, the pentecost is a most joyous space for conferring baptisms; wherein, too, the resurrection of the Lord was repeatedly demonstrated among the disciples, and the hope of the advent of the Lord indirectly pointed to. ... However, every day is the Lord's; every hour, every time, is apt for baptism: if there is a difference in the solemnity, distinction is there none in the grace. (*On Baptism*, 19; *Ante-Nicene Fathers* 3:678)

This baptismal use of the *pentecost* lead to its further development in the fourth- and fifth-century church. Already in Tertullian's time the night of the paschal vigil was coming to be regarded as the central time for Christian baptism. New Christians were immersed into Christ's death on this night of all the stories, centering in the story of his cross. New Christians were added to the community on this festival of the community's identity. The tendency to make *pascha* the time for baptisms was heightened after the legalization of Christianity. But then the fifty days became immensely important as a time to talk with the newly baptized about the mysteries of baptism and of the eucharist that they had now experienced. "Mystagogy" was the name given to such teaching. Situated in the old time of paschal rejoicing, mystagogy could not be reduced to technical introductions to sacramental practice. It had to be a leading into the mystery of the presence of the risen Lord in the assembly around the word, the bath, and the meal.

What one should note in all of this early history of the festival is that Easter was not a little historical drama, acting out what happened to Jesus. Rather, it was a proclamation of God's mercy in Christ, present now, saving the people and transfiguring the times. Passover was an ancient feast of the identity and hope of the people. Because Jesus was killed at Passover, Christians saw Passover itself as transformed. Their *pascha* was about the identity and hope of the church—and of all peoples and all things—in Christ. It was for all the identifying stories, told now as centered in Christ. It was for baptism.

This then is the pattern of the Easter observance that our churches have inherited: all the deliverance stories at *pascha* and the rejoicing in the deliverance of the people throughout the fifty days; the cross at the paschal vigil and the encounter with the resurrection throughout the *pentecost*; baptism at the great night that begins Easter and mystagogy throughout the whole of Eastertide; and the whole, *pascha* and *pentecost*, as an eighth day to the year, a word of overflowing grace, a taste of the *eschaton*, a mark of Christian identity and an occasion for Christian assembly.

MYSTAGOGY: THE PRESENT STRUCTURE OF EASTER PREACHING

This pattern of Easter is a pattern we can still use. Our tendency, of course, is to accentuate the ancient Christian insight that every day, every time is the Lord's and that every place is a place to know that the crucified one is risen. But we would be foolish not to see that our weeks—as well as our years—need a Sunday. These festivals are for us, not God. Our access to the truth of the resurrection needs the assembly of the community, the use of the Scriptures, the "breaking of bread," and the faithful, witnessing word of our brothers and sisters. Days and seasons have developed among us as means of assembly and means of proclamation. The transformation of *pascha* and the *pentecost* to be bearers of the gospel of Jesus Christ is, after the Christian use of Sunday, the oldest of these days and seasons. And it is a good gift.

But even when we make use of the festivals to illuminate all our days, our tendency is to historicize them. Taking up an amalgam of Lukan and Johannine chronologies, we turn the feasts into occasions to remember something that happened away from here and now. On Easter, Christ rose. On the following Sunday, he was seen by Thomas. On the fortieth day he ascended. On the fiftieth day he poured out the Spirit.

Such a historical memory is not wrong. In the ancient church—and in the current lectionary—there has been some use of the correspondence between annual dates and historic events. Passover came to be Christianized into *pascha*/Easter in the first place because Jesus was killed at Passover-time. The events of the gospel occurred in this world, in our real history.

But historicization is simply not deep enough, not useful enough to faith, not responsible enough with the original purpose of Christian feasts. It can seem to put Christian meaning away from us, somewhere else, away from here. And it forgets the church, "that wonderful and sacred mystery," which, for all its brokenness, is the very place now where access to the risen one is promised. "I am with you always," the risen one says to the church (Matt. 28:20).

The alternative to historicization sees the festivals as existing in our time. Easter and Eastertide are for us and for all the needy ones of the present world, that we may believe. Jesus Christ was crucified once-for-all, long ago. His resurrection is forever true. But the festivals make use of the rhythms of time to proclaim this to us, in our own place and time. Easter makes use of the old springtime deliverance festival to tell again the deliverance that is in Christ's cross. Easter gives us the occasion to immerse new Christians into that deliverance and to remember and live from our own immersion. The fifty days use the old *laetissimum spatium* to gather us, now, deeper into the overflowing mystery of Christ's resurrection. He is risen. So are we. He pours out the Spirit. That Spirit is alive in our meeting. By the Spirit, the risen one encounters us with mercy now, in word and meal and needy neighbor. His wounded hands show us that our death is even now transformed. He is ascended to be everywhere with such transforming love. He is ascended to be with us, ascended into the sacraments. The whole of the story of his resurrection is the pouring out of the living Spirit, so the final day, the fiftieth day, called now "Pentecost" or "Whitsunday," is not a new thing, another historical reminiscence. It is a summary of all the fifty days, poured out into our hearts, giving grounds for the ongoing life of the church.

The lectionary for the fifty days of Easter is structured so as to make this conception of the festival clear. The Gospel readings for the Sundays of year A, largely drawn from John, are almost all words and stories that intend to provide a framework in which the present community, which has "not seen," can yet "come to believe" (John 20:29, Second Sunday). Indeed, all the readings exist so that we may "understand the Scripture" (John 20:9, First Sunday; cf. Luke 24:27, 32, Third Sunday) by encountering now the risen Christ. The Gospel for the Eighth Sunday ("Pentecost") makes clear the identity between this resurrection encounter and the out-

pouring of the Spirit. It is a story from the "first Easter" or from an antici-
pation of that day in which the Spirit proceeds from the heart and mouth of
the crucified and risen Christ (John 20:19-23 or John 7:37-39).

But while the first three Sundays and the Eighth Sunday make use of
"resurrection stories" for the purposes of the season, the Fourth, Fifth,
Sixth, and Seventh Sundays use other stories for the same purposes. Here
we meet the Good Shepherd (John 10:1-10, Fourth Sunday) and the Christ
of the Farewell Discourse (John 14–17, Fifth through Seventh Sundays).
What we need to recall is that in the Fourth Gospel the words of all the discourses correspond to the content of the great Johannine "signs." The
Gospel itself proceeds through alternating signs and discourses up to the
great discourse of John 13–17 and the great sign of John 18–20. Meeting
Christ in the discourses (e.g., the "bread of life" discourse, John 6:25-59)
is the same as meeting Christ in the signs to which they correspond (e.g.,
the multiplication of loaves, John 6:1-14). But the sign to which John 10
and John 14–17 correspond is none other than the greatest one: Jesus'
going away and coming again, his death and resurrection. The discourses
are not historical remembrances; they give us words in which to meet the
crucified and risen one now.

That such a sense of the meaning of the *pentecost* is an ecumenical trea-
sure is clear when we compare these Gospel readings of the current Western church with the traditional Sunday Gospel readings for the fifty days
found in the Eastern (or Orthodox) church's *pentecostarion.* There the
assembly reads the Johannine prologue on the First Sunday—as if only
now, in the resurrection, could the community receive the "grace upon
grace" that flows from the fullness of the incarnation (John 1:16)—and
from John 7 on the Eighth Sunday—to make clear the source and meaning
of the "Spirit." On the Second and the Seventh Sundays the readings are
just as in the Western church: Thomas (John 20) on the Second, the "High
Priestly Prayer" (John 17) on the Seventh. In between, the Eastern church
uses a series of Johannine readings that image overwhelming and healing
encounters with Christ by women and by men—by the "myrrh-bearing
women" on the Third Sunday (Mark 15:43-16:8), by the paralytic at the
pool on the Fourth (John 5:1-15), by the Samaritan woman at the well on
the Fifth (John 4:5-42), and by the man born blind and sent to the pool on
the Sixth (John 9:1-38).

People who know the current Western lectionary will recognize here the
baptismal themes and images that have come to strongly characterize our
readings in Lent, in the time that turns toward and prepares for *pascha* and
the *pentecost.* But preachers who must preach on the Western readings
during the great fifty days may also find in the East an interpretive key to
help unlock the use of our Gospel pericopes: All the texts are to be

preached so that the people—women and men—come to the risen Christ
now—come like the woman at the well or the man born blind—and
receive from his fullness grace upon grace.

This purpose is also clear in the other readings of the Easter lectionary.
The first lesson of our current lectionaries (including the Eastern *pentecostarion*) is usually from the Acts of the Apostles. The point is not to
make us wish for the "time of miracles" in the church but rather to present
the church itself, with all its failings, as a place where the risen Christ acts.
Alternatively, the lectionary of the *Book of Common Prayer* presents a
series of major readings from the Hebrew Scriptures that recover an
ancient paschal theme by celebrating God's repeated deliverance of the
people. The second lesson in our lectionaries is almost always drawn from
a nearly continuous reading of 1 Peter. This latter book has sometimes
been considered to be an ancient paschal baptismal catechesis. Whether or
not this account of the origin of the book is accurate, 1 Peter can function
as mystagogical catechesis for us, leading us more deeply into the meaning
of the resurrection, into the life of those who have been born anew (1 Peter
1:3, Second Sunday) in baptism and tasted the goodness of the Lord (1
Peter 2:3, Fifth Sunday) in the eucharist.

Indeed, one way to sum up the purpose of the lectionary for Eastertide,
the purpose that needs to come to expression in Easter preaching, is to
call it *mystagogy*. In the fifty days, the preacher, faithfully using the materials of the pericopes, leads those who have been baptized—at *pascha* or
at any time, for the paschal baptism gathers to itself the remembrance and
reality of all baptizing!—deeper into the mystery of the resurrection and
the mystery of the identity of the church as these are known in the sacraments. At the same time and in the same movement, by making clear who
the risen Christ is, the preacher also invites all the world, including those
who have *not* been baptized, to "come to him, a living stone" (1 Peter
2:4, Fifth Sunday).

Another way to sum up Easter preaching is to use the scheme so promi-
nent in the Fourth Gospel, the primary source for the readings of the season. If the great "sign" of Easter, the sign to which all the other Johannine
signs have pointed, is the death and resurrection of the Lord, then preaching is to be a "discourse" to that sign. This discourse is to say and be, in
words, what the sign is and reveals. *Pascha* and the eucharist of every
Sunday give us the sign. Preaching throughout the fifty days makes that
sign available in words. Easter preaching is to be the crucified and risen
Christ, the Christ of the eucharist, existing in our midst as *speech*.

Preaching the resurrection does not mean sermons without room for
sin, sorrow, death, loss, hurt. It is said of Pope Leo the Great that he
preached on the death of Christ four times during the great and holy week:

once on Palm Sunday, once each on both Wednesday and Friday, and *once on Easter Day itself.* To preach the risen Christ is also to preach the suffering and slain one. The wounds in John 20 make that clear: the resurrection has not caused the disappearance of those marks of death. Then, where Christ's cross is, there is room for all sorrow and there is power for its transformation.

On eight Sundays—and on Ascension Day—then, preachers give voice to the resurrection amid the truth of our present world and the truth of our need. Preachers do this so that we might have words to enable our faith, to newly name our identity, to understand what baptism is and to anchor our year. In many ways this task is no different than the task of preaching on any Sunday, any "eighth day." But in Easter, the task is especially solemn and festive: the great annual observance is to be brought into words, the words are to be words to interpret our year and all our years. That is a daunting task. But preachers must not be afraid. The very risen one, who is the heart and meaning of all these texts, says, in prayer for apostolic preachers, "Now they know that everything you have given me is from you; for the words that you gave to me I have given to them" (John 17:7-8, Seventh Sunday). God grant that it may be those words we speak!

In the material that follows, consideration begins with the *Gospel* reading of the Sunday or festival as the key reading of the set of pericopes and as the principal preaching text. In the Sunday assembly, the Gospel text always stands for Jesus Christ risen. But this text is not read alone; it has a context. It is read after two other readings and a sung psalm. It is read in Easter's fifty days and in the assembly's liturgy. So there follows, in succession, consideration of the *first lesson* (from Acts or from the Old Testament), the *Psalm* (which is sung as a way to receive and celebrate the first lesson, communally proclaiming yet another biblical text), and the *second lesson* (mostly from 1 Peter). In each case, these texts are considered in themselves. But they are also considered in context, as their meaning is emphasized, extended, and transformed in the church by juxtaposition to the other readings and to the celebration of Easter. The consideration of each Sunday's texts is then concluded with a brief exposition of some part of the Easter *liturgy*—songs and actions widely characteristic of Christian celebration in the fifty days. These expositions can only serve as evocations of the full assembly action that always surrounds Scripture reading and preaching and that is part of the concern of preaching. In order to preach, the preacher must fill out such evocations with a fuller and detailed knowledge of the local liturgy and local congregation and of their setting within events in the larger community and world.

Easter Day
The Resurrection of our Lord

Lectionary	First Lesson	Psalm	Second Lesson	Gospel
Revised Common	Acts 10:34-43 *or* Jer. 31:1-6	Ps. 118:1-2, 14-24	Col. 3:1-4 *or* Acts 10:34-43	John 20:1-18 *or* Matt. 28:1-10
Episcopal (BCP)	Acts 10:34-43 *or* Exod. 14:10-14, 21-25; 15:20-21	Ps. 118:14-29	Col. 3:1-4 *or* Acts 10:34-43	John 20:1-10 (11-18) *or* Matt. 28:1-10
Roman Catholic	Acts 10:34, 37-43	Ps. 118:1-2, 16-17, 22-23	Col. 3:1-4 *or* 1 Cor. 5:6-8	John 20:1-9
Lutheran (LBW)	Acts 10:34-43	Ps. 118:1-2, 15-24	Col. 3:1-4	John 20:1-9 (10-18) *or* Matt. 28:1-10

GOSPEL: JOHN 20:1-9 (10-18); MATTHEW 28:1-10

The Gospel for this first of the fifty days is the Johannine account of the
empty tomb, or it is that account combined with the appearance to Mary
Magdalene. Where local assemblies have a choice, they would do well to
read the longer text. In either case, this first part of the four presentations
of the resurrection in John (the tomb, Magdalene, the disciples, Thomas—
a fifth presentation, at the lake, is in the appendix, John 21) is read now as
the initial text for our Easter preaching. It is read here in order that the
principal text on Easter Day might be paired with the principal text read on
Good Friday, the Johannine passion (John 18–19), and that thereby the full
witness of the Fourth Gospel might be heard at this center of Christian celebration. It is not read in order to make us marvel at the distant "miracle of
the empty tomb," but rather to invite us to listen to the Scripture now and
believe (20:9), hearing ourselves called by name (20:16).

The text presents us, first of all, with the heightened inaccessibility of
Jesus. What he said is true: "You will look for me; and . . . 'Where I am
going, you cannot come'" (13:33). Indeed. He is dead. More: "They have
taken the Lord out of the tomb, and we do not know where they have laid
him" (20:2). The seeker cannot even find the shards of his former presence, his former bodily accessibility (20:13, 15). But then there follows, in
the midst of this desolation, faith (20:8), the potential witness of the Scriptures (20:9), the calling and naming voice (20:16), and the return to the
community as the appropriate locus for his transformed availability
(20:17-18). Thus, we know the truth also of the other word of Jesus: "I will
come again and will take you to myself" (14:3).

Here—and in the following passage, John 20:19-29—the Fourth
Gospel carefully unites communal appearances with accounts of epipha-
nies to individuals. Elsewhere, these different kinds of stories are kept
quite separate (Mark 16:1-8; Luke 24:13-49; cf. Acts 9:1-9; Rev. 1:9-20).

But this is the Gospel that can tell unique stories of individuals (Nicodemus, the woman at the well, the man born blind) as models for communal activity, and can link eschatological promises stated in the singular (12:25-26) to the promised universal drawing of all to Christ (12:32). So also here the appearances to Mary Magdalene and to Thomas—and the interaction of Peter and the Beloved Disciple with the tomb—send the individuals toward the community or arise within the community, and provide a model for all believers. At the same time, the very importance of these unique stories makes clear that the community around the risen Christ is not a crowd, a faceless mass, an exercise in "groupthink." Each one, in uniqueness, is called to faith. John's Gospel features a late antique tendency to religious individualism but transforms it into a rich personal/communal vision of the church.

The pericope before us has its clear function within the Fourth Gospel. Together with the rest of chapter 20, it completes the account of the great sign of Jesus' "hour" (13:1), the sign of his death and resurrection, toward which the whole Gospel has been moving and for which chapters 13–17 have provided the corresponding discourse. This summary sign is presented—as are all the signs (20:30-31)—so that the hearers or readers of the Gospel might believe and live. In the very presentation, however, the means of coming to such faith and the authoritative witnesses to the faith are revealed.

As with all Johannine materials, very concrete details, details that seem sure to anchor us in the concrete earth, are combined with the symbolic and the abstract. Thus, the reports of the places of the discarded grave-clothes (20:5-7) and of the presence of the seeming "gardener" (20:15) are combined with the timing "while it was still dark" (20:1) and the difficult speech about ascension (20:17). The darkness almost certainly is intended symbolically: here is that darkness of death and falsehood into which the true light shines (cf. 1:5 and *passim*). The discussion about ascension is surely intended to help the hearers understand that Jesus is not available any longer by direct touch, but, in a transformed but still bodily way, by new means. Nonetheless, these characteristic Johannine usages should not mislead the interpreter to spend a lot of time also trying to figure out the "meaning" of the placement of the linens or whether the risen one, in a lovely poetic turn, is here presented as the "gardener" of God's paradise. These concrete details are probably presented as just that: indications that this story has to do with the earth, with our actual lives—with the actual inaccessibility of the dead, for example! Neat grave clothes and empty tombs do not bring me face to face with my beloved dead.

Similarly, fragments in the pericope make it clear that John is reworking material we have known from the Synoptic Gospels. Thus, the removed stone (20:1), the plural "we" (20:2) and the angels (20:12) recall earlier forms of the story in which the placing of the stone was actually recounted (Mark 15:46; Matt. 27:60, 66), Mary came with other women who could make up the "we" (Mark 16:1; Luke 24:10,22), and the angels had a continuing narrative function, a message to deliver (Mark 16:6-7; Luke 24:4-7, 23). None of these fuller forms are present in the Fourth Gospel. But the interpreter should not then be misled into easily assuming that the meaning of the pericope lies in the critique or transformation that John applies to the Synoptic material. Rather, the means of coming to faith in the risen one—the means with which the pericope is most deeply concerned—are seen as situated within the traditional stories of the churches. Those stories are assumed, received. Peter is here. So is the Magdalene. Also the angels and the community. All of them are made to be witnesses to the means to faith.

What are these means? For the Fourth Gospel, in this penultimate pericope, faith is enabled by the story of Jesus—and now, especially, the story of his resurrection—told as a "sign." It is told as an invitation to and grounds for faith, as an encounter with the meaning of Jesus, with his glory and grace, and as the dawning of Jesus' own "hour." Moreover, that story-as-sign is a means to faith when it is told within *the community*, grounded in the witness of *the beloved disciple*, understood as in accord with God's intention in the *Scripture*, and heard as the very *voice of Jesus* calling his own by name.

This pericope then brings to fruition and summary the Johannine intention with the "signs," an intention that began with Cana (2:11)—and, even earlier, with "we have seen his glory . . . full of grace and truth" (1:14). Moreover, along with John's disciples and Nathanael (1:35-39, 46) and many others throughout the book, the pericope invites anyone who wishes to know the truth of the signs to come to the community, to "come and see." The community of this invitation in the Fourth Gospel is the one that sees itself as founded on the witness of the "beloved disciple," a witness with which the book is filled (13:23; 18:15; 19:26-27, 35; cf. 1:35, 40; 21:24; 1 John 1:1) as a special, privileged, and bodily witness, even though the community does not wish to see itself as cut off from Peter or the others either. So here, the beloved disciple comes first to the tomb and believes first, while yielding primacy of entrance—obvious, public primacy—to Peter.

The means for coming to faith are signs, community, witness of the beloved disciple, and *Scripture*. For, while the beloved disciple believes without yet understanding the Scripture (20:9), the community now has *both* the witness of that disciple, enfleshed in the book of the Gospel, and the ancient Scriptures themselves, newly understood as bearing witness to

Christ (1:45; 2:22; 5:39, 46; 7:38; 12:16; 19:28, 36-37; cf. 1:14). The community is able to gather around both the Scriptures and the Gospel, working together. Indeed, for the community, the risen one is that word, lamb, temple, holy name, well, manna, flowing river, shepherd, vine of which one may *hear* in the Scriptures but that one now encounters in him. Jesus Christ is the meaning of the Scriptures.

Like Mary, the person who is coming to believe hears the voice of the risen one calling his own by name: "He calls his own sheep by name. . . . they know his voice" (10:3-4). For the Fourth Gospel, neither the empty tomb nor even the angels speak that voice, but the risen one himself. He then directs Mary and all those who hear her story to the community, the place where her witness—as the testimony of the "apostle to the apostles"—and the witness of the beloved disciple and the new understanding of the Scriptures will now be treasured. There, in those very means, the voice of the risen one is heard, calling each by name, and so "there will be one flock, one shepherd" (10:16). There, in the community, there will be a new way of touching him by seeing and touching his wounds in faith (20:27).

As those in this community are coming to know him risen, an astonishing thing happens. It was not just the dead Jesus who was inaccessible. It was *God*: "You have never heard his voice or seen his form. . . . You know neither me nor my Father" (5:37; 8:19). But now the risen one, who calls Mary by name and sends her to the community, says of God: "my Father and *your* Father . . . my God and *your* God" (20:17). To come to know him risen, to hear his voice, to receive his word is to come to know the living God (cf. 14:6-10, 23).

Read on Easter Day, this text invites the preacher to tell the truth about death, darkness, and the inaccessibility of Jesus and God. In that sense, it provides a possibility to "preach the cross" on Easter Day, together with Leo the Great (see the Introduction, p. 11). This text knows darkness, loss, weeping, seeking and not finding. At the same time, the preacher is invited to make use of the same means that the Fourth Gospel uses—means that are still alive in the community today—to speak a word that will be experienced by the hearers like a sign-narrative, like the very naming voice of Christ. Those means are: the Scriptures interpreted of Christ, the living witness of the Gospel book, the presence of the community, and the sacraments as a new way to see and touch the wounds of the risen one. These means need to be used not in order to "prove" the resurrection, certainly not in order to demonstrate human immortality or life-after-death or other diversions for which Easter is commonly used. Rather, they should be used so that the hearers feel themselves "known" by the terms of the text, "called by name" both by the text's intimate knowledge of human darkness and loss and by the astonishing assertion that all the fullness of God alive meets us here, ending fear and wiping away tears. The resurrection of Christ is now, and the encounter with the risen one gives both *God* and *life* again.

All the lectionaries except the Roman Catholic provide for **Matthew 28:1-10** to be read as an alternative Gospel for the day. The intention, in this case, is to forego the full Johannine witness (provided by John 20 for Easter Day paired with the Johannine passion on Good Friday), in favor of the Sunday-to-Sunday linkage of the texts from Matthew, the primary synoptic Gospel book in Year A (Matthew 28 today paired with the Matthean passion read last Sunday). The text from the Fourth Gospel, especially if the full passage is read, is the stronger choice. If, however, the Matthean text is used, the preacher should note that this passage is essentially the Markan account (Mark 16:1-8), expanded with the earthquake, the angel, the guards and, most importantly, with an actual appearance of Jesus. Unlike Mark, Matthew does not end with the silence of Mark 16:8. Just as in John, the risen one himself directs the women to the community, where they will come as first witnesses. In Matthew, just as in Mark,the "Galilee" where they are together sent is to become the place of the revelation of the abiding presence of Christ in the teaching and baptizing church (28:16-20). Read on Easter, this text will assist the assembly to hear the "Greetings!" of the risen one, to lay hold of his feet now in worship, to know that this present gathering is in "Galilee," and to be sent to bear witness.

FIRST LESSON: ACTS 10:34-43; EXODUS 14:10-14, 21-25; 15:20-21; JEREMIAH 31:1-6

The first reading begins the practice, which will be followed throughout the fifty days, of turning to the Acts of the Apostles, rather than to the Hebrew Scriptures, for the initial reading of the Liturgy of the Word. The intention, of course, is to image the churches themselves—and their mission—as loci for the activity of the risen Christ. In this case, however, the lectionary presents us with a classic Lukan sermon by Peter. The sermon itself sums up the Lukan version of the Gospel, presenting matters "orderly" (Luke 1:1, 3) and with universal appeal (Acts 10:34-35). It also testifies to the resurrection with a witness to the resurrection meals (10:41), to the commission to preach (10:42), and to the corroborating evidence of the prophetic Scriptures (10:43). The text is a summary of Lukan themes and is much like other sermons to the Gentiles found in Acts. This sermon is the last one in Acts ascribed to Peter.

Read at Easter, this text provides the assembly with a model resurrection sermon, an ancient proclamation set next to the living voice of the current preacher on this day. The present preacher will do well also to so preach the resurrection that what actually happens is the proclaiming of peace (10:36), the availability of the full story of Jesus (10:38-40), and, thereby, the announcement of the forgiveness of sins (10:43).

Read next to the Gospel for the day, an interesting thing happens. We hear now, on Easter, the literary "voice" of Peter, a voice that is absent in John 20. The Gospel depends rather on the voices of Mary Magdalene and of the beloved disciple, who are "alternative" rather than "official" sources for the constitution of the ancient church. Now, in all these witnesses as in a united chorus, we are invited to hear the calling and naming voice of the one shepherd, the center of the one church. What is more, set next to the means to faith held out by the Johannine pericope, we can see that the Acts passage gives us its parallels: the meals with the risen one, the testimony of the first witnesses, preaching, and the forgiveness of sins. This text may help the preacher to invite the current assembly to "eat and drink with him who rose from the dead" as a means available not only to ancient Peter but today available in the eucharist. This eating and drinking can be the community's transformed "touching" of the one who has ascended "to my God and your God" (John 20:17).

The Episcopal lectionary of the *Book of Common Prayer* presents **Exodus 14:10-14, 21-25; 15:20-21** as an alternative first reading. This text is a simple version of the escape of the people from Egypt—and from their fears of death—through the parting of the sea, and it concludes with the account of Miriam's song. This is, of course, the ancient story at the heart of the Passover, the festival from which the church's *pascha* has developed. In that sense, it is appropriately *the* text for Easter! While it will always be read at the Easter Vigil, when it is read on Easter Day, next to the Gospel, the text provides a marvelous example of the *Scripture* as witness to the resurrection of Christ (John 20:9). The exodus story has, throughout church history, been seen by Christians as one of the grounds for the Pauline and Nicene confession, "that he was raised on the third day in accordance with the Scriptures" (1 Cor. 15:4). The preacher may find that this grounding assists the depth of preaching. The fear of the people before Pharaoh's might can appropriately be set next to the Johannine inaccessibility of Jesus and of God. Miriam's song can richly interpret Mary's encounter. And the Exodus text, generally, provides an imagery with which to receive current agonies and to proclaim God's astonishing, life-giving mercy in Christ: the resurrection of Jesus brings us across the sea, to freedom and life. The Episcopal alternative, continuing the reading of Hebrew Scriptures as the first lesson also in Easter, may be a better way for all of us to proceed.

The Revised Common Lectionary also provides an alternative first reading from the Hebrew Scriptures for this day. **Jeremiah 31:1-6**, a poem celebrating the promised restoration of the people in the land and at Zion, is a less obvious choice for Easter than the Episcopal alternative. Nonetheless, it allows the assembly to see the resurrection of Christ as a communal joy and as a fulfillment, against all death and destruction, of the ancient "covenant sentence" of Israel: "they shall be my people and I will be their God" (cf. Jer. 31:1). Such a use of the text borrows the ancient language of hope for *return* from exile and for the *fertility* of the land to express Christian faith, believing that this text too belongs to the "Scripture" of John 20:9. Now Jesus has "survived the sword" (Jer. 31:2) and been the object of God's faithfulness (31:3), and so we all have "found grace in the wilderness" (31:2), have been loved "with an everlasting love" (31:3), have come to newly planted vineyards (31:5).

PSALM 118

The Psalm for the day is the ancient processional psalm that, as the last of the "Hallel Psalms," came to have a very strong association with the celebration of both Passover/*pascha* and the Feast of Tabernacles. It is still sung at the Jewish Passover *seder.* The psalm is one of the most obvious compositions for public liturgy to be found in the psalter, though its original situation remains obscure. At several points, its imagery influenced the composition of the story of Jesus, the development of early Christology, and the language of Christian liturgy. Sung after the first reading—whether that reading is Peter's sermon or the Exodus account or Jeremiah's poem—it sounds the Easter word, as if in the voice of Christ: "I shall not die, but live" (118:17), bringing us to respond, "This is the day that the LORD has made" (118:24).

SECOND LESSON: COLOSSIANS 3:1-4

The second lesson is a central passage from this deutero-Pauline writing. These verses provide the turn, the junction, the "therefore," between the teaching (*didache*) of the epistle and its moral exhortation (*paraenesis*). The pericope sums up the teaching already presented (3:1a, 3-4) as the basis for a sentence that summarizes in turn the ethics to follow (3:2). Given the text's situation in the epistle, it is important for the reader to understand that "things that are on earth" are *not* human existence and the body, not the cosmic "all things" that Christ has reconciled (1:15-20) and from which Christian believers are by no means removed. Rather, they are religious observance, legalism, and the submission to authorities and "elemental spirits" (2:8-23). The "things that are above" are, on the contrary, Christ, crucified and risen, as the mystery of God, and the faith and thanksgiving that are through him (1:15—2:7). From these, and not from religious observance, flow compassion, forgiveness, and the "new self" that is beyond ethnic and economic distinctions (3:5-17). To the world, Christ is dead and gone. No wonder he is "above" and "hidden," just as God is hidden.

But if our life is with Christ, where he is, then it too is "hidden." It too comes with him as a gracious gift. Our life is not secured by our observances and legalisms, by our religion and our efforts. Rather, our pervasive death is shared by Christ. We are dead with him when he was killed, and we have been baptized into that death (2:12). We are alive only with Christ, receiving "real life" by faith in the God who raised him. We are alive in the same word that presents his resurrection to us (cf. 3:16) and our life is under the same promise of final public visibility as he is (3:4). This is an utterly different conception of "resurrection" and "life with Christ" than is present in most American religion as "the belief in immortality." And it is a profound basis for Christian ethics.

Read on Easter this text may also serve as the paraenetic turn, the "so what," to our great celebration, just as it does to the epistle. It invites us away from religious attempts at immortality and the guaranteeing of life, and toward hearing the gracious word of the day. That word speaks the risen Christ so that we may live. It does not use the Easter story to prove the "spiritual" nature of humanity, the inability for human beings to die, or the ultimate reward for all striving. No. We die. Really. This text sounds the baptismal theme of Easter, asserting our death and our utter dependence on God. It then helps us to see the compassion and mutual forgiveness that flow from the Easter word as a baptismal way. Above all it may help us to know again that, for Christians, our life, our survival, and that of our dearest ones—a sort of universal subtheme on Easter—are entirely linked to Christ. We may see our true life—and the life of our dead— exactly there where we see Christ alive: in word and sacrament and in the compassionate turning to the neighbor. "The body of Christ," says the minister of communion, pressing the holy bread into our hands. Being translated ethically, this says: "End your striving. Here is your life, in Christ alive. Now turn to your neighbor in love."

Read next to the Gospel of the day, the theme of the hidden Christ in the hidden God illuminates and strengthens the Johannine theme of inaccessibility. To the world Jesus is dead, and he has indeed gathered all our experiences of death and the absence of God into himself. But then, in turn, the Johannine "means" of transformed access to the risen Lord (and so to the living God) illuminate those "things that are above" to which the Colossian hearers are invited to turn. Our celebration of Easter is invited to be such a turning to the "things which are above," to the risen body of Christ, to the Johannine "means" wherein we may say, "My Lord and my God!"

(John 20:28), rather than an observing of "festivals, new moons, or sab-baths" (Col. 2:16) for the securing of our own life.

(For 1 Corinthians 5:6-8, see below under Easter Evening.)

LITURGICAL CONSIDERATIONS

Around these texts flows *the liturgy* of the day. Indeed, a classic character-istic of the celebration of Easter day in the Western church was that the Alleluia which greeted the Gospel reading was extended in a "sequence," so that the welcoming of the Gospel text was even more festive than usual. Many such sequences, hymnlike texts that came to be set to the melismatic notes for the final *a* of *alleluia*, were sung in the medieval church, but only two have widely survived into current ecumenical usage: *Veni sancte spir-itus* for the day of Pentecost and *Victimae paschali laudes* for Easter Day and its octave. The latter is an eleventh-century text and tune, found in many hymnals today as "Christians, to the Paschal Victim," but also found in the form of the other hymns that it inspired: for example, the twelfth-century German hymn, "Christ is Arisen," the sixteenth-century Luther hymn, "Christ Jesus Lay in Death's Strong Bands," or the nineteenth-cen-tury English hymn, "Christ the Lord is Risen Today; Alleluia!"

Let this *sequence* stand for all the singing with which the lectionary readings will be surrounded today. Easter rightly calls forth the communi-ty's song and Easter Day is a great day of singing as well as preaching. In fact, the strong text of the ancient sequence itself, repeated in a variety of ways in other hymnody, reinforces much that we have seen in the texts, much that is the business of Easter preaching. At the heart is the central paradox of the crucified one, the one who tasted all loss and death: "The prince of life who died, reigns immortal." More: in the hymn, Mary Mag-dalene addresses *us*. We are the community to which she is sent. The resur-rection is a word for today: "Speak, Mary, declaring what you saw when wayfaring." Moreover, in the end, Christ is not spoken about as a distant third person. He is addressed as present. That is the resurrection. With the sense of welcoming Christ in the Gospel text, we turn and say: *"Tu nobis, victor rex, miserere"*: "Have mercy, victor king, ever reigning!"

With the texts we have considered interwoven and juxtaposed to the assembly, to the church's hymnody, to the paschal candle burning from last night, to the presence of the newly baptized and to the Easter eucharist, the fifty days have begun. The preacher is urged to bring all these things to expression, doing in contemporary words some of the magnificent things these texts are doing.

Easter Evening
The Resurrection of Our Lord

Lectionary	First Lesson	Psalm	Second Lesson	Gospel
Revised Common	Isa. 25:6-9	Psalm 114	1 Cor. 5:6b-8	Luke 24:13-49
Episcopal (BCP)	Acts 5:29a, 30-32 or Dan. 12:1-3	Psalm 114 or 136 or 118:14-17, 22-24	1 Cor. 5:6b-8 or Acts 5:29a, 30-32	Luke 24:13-35
Lutheran (LBW)	Dan. 12:1c-3 or Jonah 2:2-9	Psalm 150	1 Cor. 5:6-8	Luke 24:13-49

Three lectionaries (Revised Common, Episcopal, Lutheran) provide readings for a eucharist late in the day of Easter Sunday. With the exception of the Gospel, these readings are widely disparate. They also will probably not provide the great majority of congregations with their principal encounter with the Scriptures on this festival. Nonetheless, they are strong readings, enriching this beginning of the fifty days. And they will be important in some places. A brief comment on each of the readings may assist preachers for this late eucharist to do their task and may assist us all to see more of the meaning of Easter.

GOSPEL: LUKE 24:13-49

The Gospel provided by these three lectionaries is an obvious choice, as one of the two New Testament accounts (one in John and one in Luke) of the events on the evening of the first Easter. The Johannine account is always read as the Gospel text for next Sunday, the Second Sunday in Easter. And part of the Lukan text (the Emmaus story) will be repeated as the Gospel for the Third Sunday in Easter. (See below, in that Sunday, for more extensive comment.)

Here it is important to note, however, that this text is finally no more "about" what happened long ago in the evening than the Gospel for Easter Day is "about" what happened in the morning. They are both proclamations to *present* hearers, in this case hearers who gather in the evening like the disciples did around the table at Emmaus and in Jerusalem. But "evening" is not all that the present hearers have in common with those ancient disciples. Here, in this present assembly, the Scriptures are also read and interpreted of Christ (Luke 24:27) and the meal is held (24:30, 41-43). The text was written to help the Lukan communities know the same burning hearts (24:32), the same recognition of the risen Lord (24:31, 35) as described in the narrative. The text is now appropriately used for that same goal in our current communities. Now the proclamation of the resurrection, of peace (24:36), and the forgiveness of sins (24:47), has come here.

FIRST LESSON: ISAIAH 25:6-9; DANIEL 12:1-3; JONAH 2:2-9; ACTS 5:29A, 30-32

The Revised Common Lectionary presents us as the first reading the stunning passage from **Isaiah 25:6-9** regarding the great feast promised for all peoples at Zion to celebrate the universal rule of the LORD. This pericope is one of the principal canonical sources for the later speculation regarding "the eschatological feast." Here the universal rule of YHWH, described in Isaiah 24–26, is also seen to extend to the conquest of death itself, "the shroud that is cast over all peoples" (25:7). Read on Easter, it enables the assembly to see the resurrection of Jesus as the accomplishment of that promise, as the beginning of the wiping away of tears. The eucharist of Easter may be seen as already a taste of that "rich food," those "well-aged wines" (25:6).

The first reading in the Episcopal and Lutheran lectionaries, uses a fragment from Jewish apocalyptic material (**Daniel 12:1-3**) to celebrate God's promise of life for faithful Israel, even in the face of death. The text probably was surrounded originally with the warfare that brought Greek/Seleucid oppression to Palestine. In characteristic apocalyptic language, it announces the activity of the great angel Michael, a kind of heavenly twin of the people of Israel, and, in the face of suffering and death, it therefore announces the survival of the faithful. This passage includes the only clear reference to "resurrection" in the entire of the Hebrew Scriptures. For Christians, reading this old promise from a time of agony may serve three purposes on Easter. First, it may situate the Easter word within a world of agony, for which this fragment is an appropriate representative. Second, it may invite us to trust that the promised survival and brightness of the wise, in the midst of terrible suffering, is exactly what we encounter in Jesus: He is the "wise," who slept in the dust and now shines like the stars, leading many to righteousness. Finally, by God's great mercy, the text may hold out the same promise to those who are written in the "Lamb's book of life" (Rev. 21:27).

The lectionary of the *Book of Common Prayer* gives, as an alternative first lesson, another text from the Acts of Apostles, in keeping with the general practice of the whole list of Easter readings. **Acts 5:29a, 30-32** is, in fact, another Lukan account of a speech of Peter. Even more than the text for Easter Day above, however, this text is a simple, elegant summary of the Lukan *kerygma.* It too may stand in our assembly as a canonical resurrection sermon from the voice of Peter.

On the other hand, the alternative reading in the *Lutheran Book of Worship* is the prayer of Jonah (**Jonah 2:2-9**) from the belly of the great fish. Since the sea-swallowing and land-return of Jonah is taken by the New Testament to be a sign of the resurrection (Matt. 12:39-40), this is a remarkable and creative choice. The prayer itself, which may have had a life outside of its current folk-tale setting, is a hymn of thanksgiving, following the same pattern of dereliction and restoration we can observe in Psalms 18 and 30. The text presents Jonah as going into death—the Sea being a great ancient figure for death and chaos—and being restored to life by God's mercy. In Christian mouths, the hymn gathers up all experience of death and celebrates the resurrection of Christ, figured by the "sign of Jonah." The God of Jonah is the God of the gospel of Jesus, the God of biblical faith "who gives life to the dead and calls into existence the things that do not exist" (Rom. 4:17).

PSALM 114; 118; 136; 150

The Psalm may be **Psalm 114** (Common, *BCP*), another of the Hallel psalms of paschal use and exodus meaning, or **Psalm 118** (*BCP*; see above), or **Psalm 136** (*BCP*), the extensive and refrained thanksgiving for God's whole history of saving action, or **Psalm 150** (*LBW*), the final great doxology of the psalter. In any case, the Psalm receives the proclamation of the first reading—Daniel's Apocalyptic or Isaiah's Mountain or Jonah's Survival or Peter's Sermon—and then borrows one of Israel's strongest texts to praise the God of the resurrection of Jesus.

SECOND LESSON: I CORINTHIANS 5:6-8

The second reading contains a remarkable Pauline metaphor in which the entire Christian life is made to be a kind of "feast of unleavened bread," since Christ is the Paschal Lamb of Passover. The text ought not be seen as any sort of evidence that Christians "kept Passover" in the first century. Rather, Christ himself, in his death and resurrection, *is* the Passover and, therefore, Christians are to live as if their whole life were the succeeding octave without leaven, to live, that is, with "sincerity and truth" (5:8). The church, by this metaphor, is the bread of the festival. The pericope stands in the great biblical tradition of using "leaven" as a symbol of evil (cf. Zech. 5:5-11), although, again, there is no evidence here that Christians did not use ordinary, leavened bread also for their eucharist. Read on Easter, the text celebrates the crucified and risen one as the full content of the feast. It then turns that proclamation toward ethical paraenesis: Let the church keep the festival by telling the truth about death ("Your boasting is not a good thing," 5:6) and about God.

Second Sunday of Easter

Lectionary	First Lesson	Psalm	Second Lesson	Gospel
Revised Common	Acts 2:14a, 22-32	Psalm 16	1 Pet. 1:3-9	John 20:19-31
Episcopal (BCP)	Acts 2:14a, 22-32 or Gen. 8:6-16; 9:8-16	Psalm 111 or 118:19-24	1 Pet. 1:3-9 or Acts 2:14a, 22-32	John 20:19-31
Roman Catholic	Acts 2:42-47	Ps. 118:2-4, 13-15, 22-24	1 Pet. 1:3-9	John 20:19-31
Lutheran (LBW)	Acts 2:14a, 22-32	Ps. 105:1-7	1 Pet. 1:3-9	John 20:19-31

GOSPEL: JOHN 20:19-31

The Gospel for this Sunday is the appearance of the risen Christ to Thomas. More accurately, it is the Johannine account of the two successive weekly gatherings of the disciples on the first two Sundays of the existence of the church. Again, however, as with the first part of the chapter, this account does not intend to establish certain historical facts, but to bless "those who have not seen and yet have come to believe" (20:29), those whose meetings have continued every week as places for hearing the signs "written in this book" (20:30-31).

If, with the majority of scholars, we take John 21 to be an appendix to the Gospel, this pericope concludes the original form of the book. As such, it includes the summary of the intention of the Fourth Gospel, a two-verse discussion of the purpose of the narration of signs (20:30-31; see above, the Gospel on Easter Day). Immediately before this summary occurs the narration of the two gatherings of the disciples. As the conclusion to the book, this final narrative also must bear considerable weight in the Johannine intention. The final purpose for the existence of the book at all comes into focus here.

It is then all the more interesting that the Gospel closes with these two successive Sunday meetings of the primitive Christian assembly. The book runs toward an *ecclesial* intention, that is, it narrates signs in order that the *church*, the assembly for which the book is intended, may believe. Such an intention does not exclude individual faith. Far from it. Rather, persons coming to faith are given their appropriate locus: the community that gathers around the presence of the risen Christ. In this regard, the shape of this second half of the final chapter exactly parallels the shape of the first half: The community (or its representatives, Mary, Peter, and the other disciple) sees the signs of the resurrection (20:1-10 and 19-23); Jesus appears to an individual (Mary and Thomas; 20:11-16 and 24-28); the individual is sent to the community (20:17-18) or becomes the occasion of the blessing of a far larger community (20:29).

Like so many of the other resurrection narratives, this passage passes on to its hearers a strategy for resurrection faith. The Johannine community for which this book was written would also have been marked by continued weekly meetings on Sunday—"after eight days" and, again, "after eight days," as the old Jewish idiom and the Johannine usage (*meth' hemeras okto*; 20:26) had it. Identification with the two meetings of John 20 would not have been difficult. Furthermore, such gatherings would likely have been in a house (20:19) and been marked by greetings of peace (20:20, 21, 26) and mutual forgiveness (20:23). Inevitably, in the Johannine community, these meetings would have included the presence of this Gospel book itself and the narration of these signs. Without further seeing of the Lord, these meetings would thereby have provided the means to "come to believe" (20:29).

But then the Jesus who is thus encountered by faith is the same who was encountered by sight in the first meetings of the church. He still holds out his wounds, still gives the promised Spirit, still sends the assembly in mission. For John's Gospel, the gift of the Spirit of God did not wait for the "day of Pentecost," but is always simultaneous with Jesus' "hour," with his cross and resurrection and risen presence (7:39; 16:7; 19:30; 20:22). Furthermore, for John's Gospel the resurrection is not some special "healing" of Jesus. It is the crucified one who is encountered as risen, as the source of the Spirit, as the living God addressable and present; his wounds are held out to bring about faith from people who live in a world of death-dealing wounds. It is *this* risen one who is still encounterable in faith amidst the narrative of the signs in the weekly meeting.

Many scholars have noted that the Fourth Gospel proceeds by a kind of alternation of revelatory actions and revelatory words, of signs (Cana, the multiplication of loaves, etc.) paired with discourses (the Bread of Life discourse, etc.), until, finally, a great discourse (14–17) is paired with the greatest sign of all, Jesus' death and resurrection (18–20). In all these cases, sign and word are intended to reveal the same truth. It is fascinating, then, to see this final passage of the book recapitulate this method by the correlation of the actions of the risen one (standing in the midst, showing the wounds, breathing on the disciples) with his words (peace, sending, gift of the Spirit, gift of forgiveness, call to faith). If, indeed, the final passages of the Gospel are intended to characterize the meaning of the community's meetings, it is not too great a speculation to imagine that the use of the book itself in that meeting was thereby imagined to go paired with actions, with lively and present signs. In that case, baptism (cf. 3:22, 26; 4:1-2; 13:8-10), the communal greeting of peace, and the shared meal (cf. 6:53-56; 13:1-5) would be characterized as places to encounter—to see and touch in faith—the serving and life-giving wounds of the risen one.

A note on translation needs to be added. We do not now know what was intended by *Ioudaioi* in John: Jews? Jewish people? Judeans? Were *Ioudaioi* also among the Christians or not? How did the term function in the likely Asia Minor surroundings of community where the Fourth Gospel had its earliest home? Whatever our answer, many passages of the Fourth Gospel have been used for the purposes of a continuing and vicious anti-Semitism, and modern preachers need to vow to end the perpetuation of that use. The Easter word does indeed come to our fearful lives, freeing us (20:19), but not, in any modern sense, from "the fear of the Jews." We would do better to translate "for fear of the Judeans."

Read in Easter, this text also invites us to see our meetings character-ized by these accounts at the end of John. We meet here "eight days later" than last Sunday, Easter Day. But more important, our meetings are regu-larly "eight days later" and "eight days later." Indeed, because of the gospel of Jesus Christ, they are always on the "eighth day," the day in our time yet beyond our time. Moreover, our meetings, too, are marked by greetings of peace, words of forgiveness, the narrative of the signs, and concrete means intended to hold out the wounds of Christ to us in water, bread, and wine. In word and sign, the wounds of Christ are here. That is, we hear and see references to Jesus being dead—like all of our dead, with our own death, in a world full of wounds and death. "The body of Christ —the blood of Christ," says the liturgy, adding yet another to the list of the slain. But these wounds are turned to us, alive, for life. "Given for you," says the liturgy. The preacher is encouraged to interpret all these things as proclaiming peace to the assembly, as full of the outpoured Spirit, as already the gift of Pentecost, as places where the living God may be encountered and worshiped, as full of the possibility to believe in the risen Christ, as sending the community into the world with a word of life. The preacher may thus concretely speak the blessing to "those who have not seen and yet have come to believe."

FIRST LESSON: ACTS 2:14A, 22-32; 2:42-47; GENESIS 8:6-16; 9:8-16

The first reading presents—as did the Easter Day lectionary—another ser-mon of Peter (Acts 2:14a, 22-32). In this case, it is the sermon from the day of Pentecost brought forward now to illuminate the whole fifty days. The passage drawn from the sermon is another Lukan summary of the *kerygma* of the death and resurrection of Jesus, the kind of summary with which the Lukan sermons are so concerned. What makes this summary so unique is the use of Psalm 16 in a thoroughgoing christological sense. Jesus Christ, crucified and risen, is taken to be the "I" of the psalm, with

David, the presumed author of the psalm, speaking as a prophet (2:30). Such exegesis of the psalms is an example of the primitive Christian reading of much of the Hebrew Scripture and of the Lukan sense that the death and resurrection of Christ are written in Moses, the prophets, and the psalms (Luke 24:44).

Read in Easter, this passage from the account of the first day of Pentecost proposes to us that the gift of the Spirit is celebrated throughout the fifty days. It sets yet another early Christian model of resurrection preaching next to today's sermon. The text also makes the powerful imagery of Psalm 16 available for the interpretation of the resurrection of Christ and gives us a general sense of the origin of the way in which Christian Easter liturgy uses the psalms. In Christ's death, the despair and loss of the psalms—and with them all human experience of loss, for which the psalms have such powerful words—are gathered up. In Christ's resurrection, the promising, comforting word of God is proclaimed as trustworthy and true.

Indeed, read next to the Gospel of the day, the promise of the psalm is seen as applying not only to Christ but, in him and his "hour," to the disciples, to Thomas and to all "those who have not seen and yet have come to believe" as well. The believer speaks to the risen one standing in the midst of the church: "You have made known to me the ways of life; you will make me full of gladness with your presence" (Acts 2:28; Ps. 16:11). That knowledge of the "presence," that "gladness," come from the very Spirit poured out from the risen Christ.

The lectionary of the *Book of Common Prayer* continues its provision of an alternate first reading by proposing **Genesis 8:6-16; 9:8-16**, a text that evokes the full story of the flood by telling only two fragments of its conclusion. Those fragments are the account of the return of the dove with the olive branch and the story of the provision of the rainbow. Once again, this is a text with a great paschal history, having been used repeatedly as a pattern for the God who saves and as a type of the resurrection. It will have been read at the Great Vigil of Easter, and its use here will recall that night which inaugurated the fifty days and welcomed the newly baptized as if they had survived the flood. Read in Easter, the text enables the preacher to give depth to the human experience of loss and death within which the resurrection is proclaimed: ours is the flood. Read next to today's Gospel the passage may suggest that the olive branch and the rainbow may be glimpsed there where the community beholds Christ's wounds by faith. Indeed, the "dove" for us, bringing the promise of the end of death and chaos, is the very Spirit of the living Christ who enlivens the communal gathering.

The Roman lectionary appoints another first reading altogether (**Acts 2:42-47**), choosing to let this Sunday make use of the image of the earliest church as devoted "to the apostles' teaching and fellowship, to the breaking of bread and the prayers" (2:42), and as engaged in that breaking of bread with "glad and generous hearts" (2:46). In Easter, the gladness is easily seen as resurrection joy in the Lord, the generosity as a turning with love toward a needy world immersed in signs of death. Next to the Gospel of the day, the Acts reading prepares us to hear the Johannine characterization of the Sunday assembly, reinforcing readings and preaching ("the apostles' word"), prayers and eucharist ("the breaking of bread"), as places of encounter with the risen Christ.

PSALM 16; 118; 111; 105

The Psalm may be any one of a great variety: The Revised Common Lectionary has us sing **Psalm 16**, echoing the use in Acts 2:25-31 but placing now the full psalm in our mouths. The Roman Catholic and Episcopal lectionaries appoint the renewed use of **Psalm 118** as a kind of "eighth day" echo of last Sunday (see above on the Psalm on Easter Day). The Episcopal use also allows the alternative singing of **Psalm 111**, a hymn of praise focused on "the works of the LORD." Here, of course, those works are taken to be summarized in the resurrection of Jesus from the dead. The lectionary of the *Lutheran Book of Worship*, quite similarly, chooses the first seven verses of **Psalm 105**, which also sing the praise of the works and "marvels" of the LORD.

SECOND LESSON: I PETER 1:3-9

The lectionaries here begin the practice, which will be followed for all the Sundays of the fifty days (except the last, the Sunday of Pentecost), of reading continuously from 1 Peter. This is a letter that may be a pseudonymous work, but may also, indeed, be from Peter himself, though "through Silvanus" (5:12), a close co-worker of Paul (cf. 1 Thess. 1:1; 2 Thess. 1:1; 2 Cor. 1:19; and the references to "Silas" in Acts). If the latter understanding is the case, it would help explain the very considerable "Pauline" character of the letter. In any case, the letter is filled with baptismal and paschal themes and is quite appropriately read as "mystagogy" in the fifty days. Unsurprisingly, many scholars have thought of the letter as a baptismal homily, as if great Peter were preaching a sermon, written by a Pauline-influenced amanuensis, standing beside the baptismal bath or pool. Only now the "sermon" is a letter, sent to the churches in Asia Minor.

The pericope for this Sunday is the opening thanksgiving of the letter, phrased in the manner of a *berakah*, a blessing of God for God's action of salvation (cf. 2 Cor. 1:3ff.). It is this genre of thanksgiving/blessing, drawn from the great tradition of Jewish prayer but now made to focus especially on the eschatological deed of God in Christ, which came to form Christian prayer so powerfully. Here, the thanksgiving is both for the resurrection of Christ and for the "new birth into a living hope" (1:3) which comes about through that resurrection. This "birth" should probably be taken to be *baptismal*, along with many other images of the letter ("sprinkled with his blood," 1:2; "purified your souls," 1:22; "born anew," 1:23; "like newborn infants," 2:2; "once you were not a people, but now you are God's people," 2:10). Indeed, the letter sees baptism as directly corresponding to the death and resurrection of Christ (3:18-21): baptism "now saves you . . . through the resurrection of Jesus Christ" (3:21).

The hope and the inheritance, the salvation, praise and honor, which faith and baptism give, are, like the risen Christ himself, hidden. They will be revealed when he is revealed (1:7). This assertion, much like the baptismally founded assertion we saw in the second lesson for Easter Day (Col. 3:1-4), is a call to faith and to Christian ethics, including endurance. It proposes that "home" for these "exiles" (1:1, 17) is where Christ is.

Read at Easter, this baptismal homily/letter invites us to faith and to the manner of life that the letter will discuss on the coming Sundays. Our baptism has given us a "home" in the risen Christ, beyond all fear and striving. Read next to the Gospel of the day, the words "although you have not seen him, you love him" (1:8) stand out in brilliance and become part of the blessing of those who do not see, yet believe. Furthermore, the baptismal focus of the letter may serve to reinforce baptism itself as one of the places where the community may encounter the Christ who is our home.

LITURGICAL CONSIDERATIONS

The liturgy in which these readings will be situated, the liturgy of Easter's fifty days, will have one great characteristic shared by all those churches that have been recovering the ancient tradition of baptizing at the Easter Vigil: it will be marked especially by the presence of the newly baptized. This presence causes the readings to be heard with new intensity by us all. Here are those who have seen in faith and cried out to Christ, "My Lord and my God!" Here are those who have survived the flood: the olives promised by the olive branch have been smeared on their brow. Here are those who have been born anew to a living hope (1 Peter), whose "boundary lines have fallen . . . in pleasant places" (Ps. 16:6). Seeing that these words are true, especially of adults who have come to faith and been baptized at Easter in our midst, we see also that they are true of all the baptized; true, indeed, of *us*. In the midst of so many signs of homelessness and death, the preacher has on this Sunday an astonishing array of images with which to speak the promise and the blessing.

Third Sunday of Easter

Lectionary	First Lesson	Psalm	Second Lesson	Gospel
Revised Common	Acts 2:14a, 36-41	Psalm 116:1-4, 12-19	I Pet. 1:17-23	Luke 24:13-35
Episcopal (BCP)	Acts 2:14a, 36-47 or Isa. 43:1-12	Psalm 116 or 116:10-17	I Pet. 1:17-23 or Acts 2:14a, 36-47	Luke 24:13-35
Roman Catholic	Acts 2:14a, 22-33	Ps. 16:1-2, 5, 7-11	I Pet. 1:17-21	Luke 24:13-35
Lutheran (LBW)	Acts 2:14a, 36-47	Psalm 16	I Pet. 1:17-21	Luke 24:13-35

GOSPEL: LUKE 24:13-35

The Gospel for this third Sunday in the fifty days is the account of the appearance of the risen Christ to the disciples on the way to Emmaus. It is read here to invite its hearers also to understand the Scriptures and to recognize the risen one in the breaking of the bread.

Luke's Gospel organizes its account of the resurrection into three parts: the tomb, Emmaus, the gathered disciples. This organization pays especial attention to the Lukan symbolic geography. The first story establishes Jerusalem as the place of death and unbelief (24:11). The Emmaus story, then—moving away from Jerusalem in despair (24:17)—establishes a word that is brought back to Jerusalem (24:33, 35). This word—together with that of Peter (24:34) and accompanied by the very presence of the risen one (24:36)—transforms Jerusalem into the new center of the worldwide mission (24:47). The longed-for "redemption of Jerusalem" (2:38), the recovery of its role in the plan of God, comes about surprisingly, from outside of Jerusalem, as Jesus himself comes from outside of Jerusalem.

The role the Emmaus story plays in Luke, then, is analogous to the role played by the appearances to Mary and to Thomas in John. All three play a mediating role, establishing a word that is sent to the larger community. But the way the Lukan account carries out this function is unique. In Luke Jesus interprets the Scripture (24:27), then takes the role of the host at the table and is recognized in the bread-rite that begins the meal. This rite, characteristic of Jewish meal-practice of the time, has already been mentioned in the accounts of the last supper (22:19) and the feeding of the multitude (9:16). This rite, combined with the wine-rite at the conclusion of the Jewish meal, became the Christian eucharist. The term "breaking of the bread" here (24:35) and in Acts (Acts 2:42; cf. 2:46; 20:7, 11; 27:35) is probably a figure of speech, a synecdoche, not just for the bread-rite, including the prayer that "blesses" God, but for the whole eucharist. The experience of recognizing Jesus in this rite then becomes the key to recognize the meaning of the "opening" of the Scriptures (Luke 24:32).

So the risen one is known in Scripture and in the meal. Otherwise, he is out of sight (24:31) or an unrecognized stranger (24:16). But Scripture "opened," that is, interpreted of the death and resurrection of Christ, and the meal, the *klasis tou artou* of Christ, belong to all the Lukan communities, not just to the Emmaus road. Scripture—or the apostolic teaching of Scripture—and a meal are found in the following Jerusalem gathering (24:41-43, 44-45), in the continuing Jerusalem community (Acts 2:42), in the gathering at Troas (Acts 20:7-11). Indeed, this last gathering shows great parallels to Emmaus: on *Sunday* the pattern is *word followed by meal*, and the whole is a gathering "to break bread" (20:7), just as "the breaking of bread" can be the report of the whole of Emmaus's meaning (24:35).

But then our pericope calls to be understood as another presentation of strategy for resurrection faith. Read by the first readers of the Luke-Acts work this passage would have been seen as a characterization of the Sunday assemblies of the Lukan churches. Those gatherings had Scripture and the meal. Then—Luke is saying—let that Scripture, Moses and the prophets and the psalms, be opened to speak of Christ and of the mission to the world. Let the meal be held, giving the community the key with which to understand the Scriptures. In both, word and meal together, let the community behold and recognize the risen Christ, showing his hands and feet (24:40), calling to faith out of fear, and transforming both the community itself and its surrounding geography.

Read at Easter, this text intends to do the same work for us. We ought not hear this witness to the resurrection and say, in the words of the old gospel song, "Oh! How I wish I could have been with them then!" Faith was no easier amid that fear and that invisibility of the Lord. We, too, have the Scripture and the meal, every Sunday. (If our eucharistic practice is not every Sunday, Luke will encourage us to change). This text—together with so many of the resurrection narratives—calls us to do *mystagogy* again with our congregation this Easter, to open up the meaning of the mysteries of word and sacrament to the baptized people who are participating in them. So, open the Scripture again to speak of God's life-giving mercy amid our death, and bless God over the bread and cup, giving this food away to show forth the victory of the resurrection amid our fears. Then see our own geography transformed to be the sacred geography of mission.

FIRST LESSON: ACTS 2:14A, 36-47; 2:22-33; ISAIAH 43:1-12

The first reading begins with the same sermon of Peter on the day of Pentecost that served as the first lesson last Sunday, by letting the final verse of the sermon (2:36) stand for the whole. The pericope then continues with a further Lukan/Petrine summary (2:38-39), with the great response to the sermon in baptism and formation of the early community (2:40-41), and with the ongoing life of that community (2:42-47). This last part of the passage functioned as the first lesson in the Roman Catholic lectionary last Sunday (see above) and will function as the first lesson in the Revised Common Lectionary next Sunday (see below). The pericope creates the Lukan ideal image of church formation by painting a picture of people joining the earliest company in Jerusalem on the day in which, according to Luke, the mission of the church was empowered by the Spirit.

Read in Easter, the text announces that the crucified one has been made "both Lord and Messiah" (2:36). It therefore holds out again the promise of God's life-giving mercy to "all who are far away" (2:39), that is, to all people, everyone who lives amid fear and death (2:25-28), finally also to us. Indeed, this same promise is also to those people for whom we often have such great fear—to our children.

Read next to the Gospel of the day, the text offers the very image of the assembly around word ("the apostles' teaching") and meal ("the breaking of bread") to which the Emmaus account gives dramatic content. The characterization of the church in Acts 2:42 ought still be true of our assemblies as well, but the *reason* for that characterization can be seen in the Gospel: opened Scripture, burning hearts, the recognition of the Lord, the end of death and fear.

The first lesson in the Roman Catholic lectionary, on the other hand, takes up the passage (**Acts 2:14, 22-33**) that was used as the first lesson in all the other lectionaries last Sunday (see above), making the promise of Psalm 16 correspond to the resurrection as encountered both at Emmaus and in the present Sunday assembly.

The Episcopal lectionary continues its practice of proposing an alternate first lesson from the Hebrew Scriptures by appointing **Isaiah 43:1-12**. This is the magnificent poem from Second Isaiah that celebrates Israel's promised return from exile as if it were a new exodus and a new creation, in which the people are saved through flood and fire and formed into God's own people. Indeed, for the poem, the return makes the blind and deaf Israel (cf. Isa. 42:18-20) see and hear and thus become God's witness.

Although this text has a much less extensive paschal history, it may be used, like the accounts of the exodus and the survival of Noah, to recount the pattern of God's salvation proclaimed among us in Christ. The Christian community borrows this language to speak of Jesus' death and resurrection: he is brought through the waters; he is loved by God and called by name; he is the proof of the living God against the tyranny of the nations, including that Roman tyranny which put him to death; those who believe in him are gathered together and made God's witnesses. Read at Easter, the text again gives us deeply resonant images with which to describe the human condition—fear, the waters, the fire, blindness and deafness, the oppressive nations—and the life-giving mercy of God: "I have called you by name, you are mine" (43:1). It sees both the risen Christ and those who believe in him as under the promise given to those who return from exile. Indeed, the baptized, also, together with Christ risen, have passed through the waters and been called by name.

Read next to the Gospel for the day, the healed blindness and deafness of the people stand forth in new clarity. Those who were deaf *hear* the meaning of the Scriptures. Those who were blind *see* the risen Christ in the holy meal. They are made God's witnesses to life (43:10; cf. Luke 24:48) in the midst of the oppressions and pretensions of the nations.

PSALM 16; 116

The Psalm, once again, may be one of a variety of choices. The Roman Catholic lectionary answers its reading of Acts 2:25ff., the Lukan quotation from **Psalm 16**, with the communal use of Psalm 16 as the Responsorial Psalm (see above on the Psalm for the Second Sunday in Easter). The Lutheran lectionary has followed this very choice, not because the corresponding passage from Acts is being read but because that psalm is such a fine celebration of God's victory over death. "The apostle's teaching and fellowship, the breaking of bread and the prayers" (Acts 2:42) do indeed show us "the path of life" (Ps. 16:11; Lutheran antiphon). The Episcopal and Revised Common Lectionaries, on the other hand, choose **Psalm 116**. This is one of the Hallel Psalms, so widely used at Passover and *pascha*, and, in this case, one that celebrates God's deliverance from death. In addition, since this is the text that names "the cup of salvation," it is appropriately sung on this Sunday of mystagogy, amidst readings in which the eucharist is seen at the heart of the life of the church.

SECOND LESSON: I PETER I:17-23

The second reading continues the presentation of this baptismal letter, which, in this case, begins to show the ethical themes that flow from the resurrection gift. Throughout the letter, "exile" and "home" remain as important subthemes. These will be themes immediately recognizable to those who have looked at Isaiah 43 as a potential first lesson. The Israel of the exile and the "dispersion" (1 Peter 1:1) have been promised return. Here this language is borrowed to characterize Christian communities. These people have been "ransomed from the futile ways" (1:18) of pagan religions to be gathered into the people of God (cf. 2:10) and so under the promise of return. Though this has happened through "the precious blood of Christ" (1:19), there is no clear theory of atonement here. It is simply so that Christ was revealed at this "end of the ages" (1:20), and that through him these former pagans have come to trust in the living and true God who raised this one who was so cruelly killed. What that resurrection gives, through Christ and the baptism into him, is faith and hope in God! The ethics that flow from this gift involve a life of "reverent fear" (1:17) before the living God, the abandonment of religion (1:18), and "genuine mutual love" (1:22) within the community.

Read at Easter, the text invites our Easter celebration to begin to turn toward ethical consequence: the end of "religion" and the renewal of genuine mutual love. Read next to the Gospel of the day, the text may help us see that the encounter with the risen Christ in word and sacrament intends to make possible in us a lively faith and hope in God, the trust that God is God and that this God rescues from fear and death. The text may also enable us to sense that the community of word, baptism, and meal already begins to taste like "homecoming" to exiles.

LITURGICAL CONSIDERATIONS

In many churches, the liturgy of the fifty days, in which these readings occur, will be marked by the burning of a large *paschal candle*, prominently present near the places of word and sacrament in the midst of the assembly. The custom of the candle had its origin in the lamps that were lit to accompany prayers at night and toward dawn, to illuminate the ancient Christian vigils. Prayers came to be associated with this lamp-lighting that praised God as the light-giver and Christ as the light of the world. At Easter, at the paschal vigil, such lamp-lighting and prayer came to be especially festive. In the West, the practice of elaborate sung prayers at the lighting of this candle finally settled into the long tradition of the *Exultet*, the praise of the candle still used at the Great Vigil of Easter in many churches.

This poetic composition praises God for the night of the resurrection, the night that is itself as bright as the day, while the only light that is burning against the darkness is the candle. The candle thus comes to stand for all the light of the resurrection of Christ cast against the intense darkness of our death, evil, and need. The candle has burned beside all the readings of the Easter Vigil and has illuminated the baptisms, themselves a kind of coming to the light. The candle has burned near the first Easter eucharist. In the *Exultet*, the cantor or deacon has prayed that this candle may still be burning when the "Morning Star" himself finally and openly comes. It is this light then that burns amidst "the apostles' teaching and the fellowship, the breaking and bread and the prayers" (Acts 2:42) of this present Sunday. It burns as if here, in the presence of Christ and his wounds, against all darkness, we exiles see him "revealed at the end of the ages" (1 Peter 1:20) for our sake, that we might come to faith. It burns near the preacher. May the preaching be full of its light.

Fourth Sunday of Easter

Lectionary	First Lesson	Psalm	Second Lesson	Gospel
Revised Common	Acts 2:42-47	Psalm 23	1 Pet. 2:19-25	John 10:1-10
Episcopal (BCP)	Acts 6:1-9; 7:2a, 51-60 *or* Neh. 9:6-15	Psalm 23	1 Pet. 2:19-25 *or* Acts 6:1-9; 7:2a, 51-60	John 10:1-10
Roman Catholic	Acts 2:14a, 36-41	Ps. 23:1-6	1 Pet. 2:20-25	John 10:1-10
Lutheran (LBW)	Acts 6:1-9; 7:2a, 51-60	Psalm 23	1 Pet. 2:19-25	John 10:1-10

In all three years of the lectionary, this Fourth Sunday of the fifty days is "Good Shepherd Sunday." Taking the place of the old *Misericordia Domini*, as the Sunday of the Good Shepherd (the Third Sunday of Easter) was known in the historic Western lectionary, this Sunday in Year A proposes to us a passage from John 10, the 23rd Psalm, and the Shepherd image from 1 Peter. On first glance, these readings do not seem to speak of the resurrection and seem like odd selections in Easter. But since ancient times, the Western church has used occasions in the fifty days to invite the assembly to encounter the risen Christ as the Shepherd who is calling his own by name, leading them into life. That life-giving voice, like the voice heard by Mary Magdalene on Easter (John 20:16; see above on Easter Day), sounds forth in the readings of the day.

GOSPEL: JOHN 10:1-10

Today's Gospel reading consists of the opening ten verses of the Good Shepherd discourse of the Fourth Gospel. These verses include the initial figure of speech (*paroimia*, John 10:6) and the first part of the following interpretation. In subsequent years, the remaining parts of the discourse will be read on this Sunday (Year B: 10:11-18; Year C: 10:22-30). While the phrase "good shepherd" does not occur in the current passage, the *paroimia* does say, "The one who enters by the gate is the shepherd of the sheep" (10:2). And "good shepherd" means essentially the same thing: "true shepherd," "real shepherd," the shepherd of the sheep and not the pretender, the destroyer.

Many scholars have argued about the location of this discourse, wondering if the earliest tradition of the Gospel book had not mismatched the passage with its context. As interesting as they are, we may leave these discussions alone, allowing the account of the healing of blindness and the subsequent controversy (9:1-41) to provide an adequate context. The man born blind is a sheep who hears the voice of the shepherd and follows him to new life. The religious leaders who reject him are examples of the "thieves and bandits" (10:1, 8, 10), the "stranger" (10:4-5).

Indeed, the parable or *mashal* (to use the Hebrew word for such a "figure of speech"; 10:6) of the sheep, the sheepfold, and the gate builds upon a great tradition in the Hebrew Scriptures. In that tradition, God is the true shepherd of Israel (Gen. 49:24; Ps. 95:7; Mic. 2:12) who acts to gather and pasture the people, especially in the face of false leadership by destroying and scattering shepherds (Jer. 23:1-4; Ezek. 34:1-22; cf. Zech. 11:4-17; 13:7-9). Such a tradition, of course, depended upon the general Near Eastern political image in which the ruling *king* could be called a shepherd. Such a practice is found in Israel also (e.g., Ezek. 34:23): David is shepherd, both literally and figuratively (were the stories of his youth, in fact, born of the figurative use of "shepherd" for his kingship?). But in the Hebrew Scriptures that leadership is frequently false. It is God who shepherds Israel. Such an assertion comes with an implied criticism of all other leadership; that is, only God is the "true king."

In John, the false and destroying "shepherds" are simply called "thieves" or "strangers." And the Johannine idea of the true shepherd seems much more dependent on the tradition of God as shepherd than on any messianic hope for a new "David." To the faith of the community of the Fourth Gospel, Jesus comes with the voice, the life, and the gathering power of God. Only, unexpectedly, unlike anything in the Hebrew Scriptures (except, perhaps, the unclear reference of Zech. 13:7-9), this shepherd *dies* for the sheep (John 10:11, 15, 17-18). Indeed, the discourse ends *both* with the assertion, "the Father and I are one" (10:30) *and* with an attempt on Jesus' life (10:31). It is appropriate to the Gospel itself, then, that the Western Christian church has found Easter a time to know the voice and life-giving presence of this shepherd who laid down his life and took it up again (10:17-18).

The "figure of speech" of 10:1-5 imagines an *aule* of the sheep, perhaps a walled and gated forecourt or yard of a small house. Then various sorts of access to the sheep, of intention with the sheep, and of mutual recognition between sheep and shepherd or false shepherds are played out in and around this fold. The interpretation of the *paroimia*, which begins at 10:7, is not unlike the appended interpretation of the Synoptic parable of the sower (cf. Mark 4:2-9, 13-20) in attributing various meanings to parts of the figure of speech itself. That Jesus is both gate and shepherd should not surprise us. Although some interpreters point to the shepherding practice in which shepherds literally make themselves the "gate," by laying down to sleep in the entrance to a sheep pen, that clever suggestion is really not necessary. Here are two different interpretations of the *paroimia* placed side by side. In the Gospel in which the "I am" sayings of Jesus draw on many images—bread, light, vine, resurrection, way, truth, life—two more are asserted here: gate or door and shepherd. These assertions are simply two ways in which the figure of speech is being allowed to work for its essential christological purpose. They are not contradictory and they do not need to be harmonized into a consistent, one-image-for-one-idea, explanation of the parable. There are, of course, further materials in the *paroimia* (the gatekeeper, for example, and the *aule* itself) that remain uninterpreted.

Our pericope includes the *paroimia* itself and the first part of the interpretation, the "I am" sayings of the gate. In the context of the Fourth Gospel, this passage serves to bring the tradition of God as shepherd to bear in understanding Jesus' mission. It also criticizes religious authority, asserts in contrast that Jesus comes for the sake of life, and begins the kind of interpretation we find in full at 14:6: "I am the way, the truth, and the life. No one comes to the Father except through me."

Read in Easter, this text makes use of *metaphor*, the wrong words used in a revelatory way, to speak to us the truth of the risen one. In fact, we have no other words but the wrong ones to say the resurrection. Jesus risen is not simply a human resuscitated. The resurrection is the encounter with the power and mercy of God under the form of its contrary. How can we say that? The particular wrong words in this text bring with them the ancient hope for God to gather, God to care for, God to rule the people. Now, in a crucified man we meet God shepherding. Read in Easter, the text cautions us against religion and religious leadership that might propose some other, destructive answer to our own death. The only way is through the body of the crucified Christ who means to bring us out to life.

This service of the crucified (cf. 13:1-5) to "his own" is surprising shepherding. It is not like the action of the mighty "shepherd"-kings of the ancient Near East. It is not even like what we might imagine as the obviously mighty rule of God, called "shepherding." And it is not the creation of immaturity and dependence—one form of destruction that religious leadership can bring—as if only the shepherd could act for the dumb sheep. But the death of Christ does call us each by name, describing us, knowing us. And the purpose of Christ's service is to bring us to life—not dependence—by bringing us to God.

Read in Easter, this text recalls the ancient mystagogy of the church. Above the oldest baptismal font modern archeology has discovered, the pool in the third-century house church in Dura Europas, Syria, there was painted an image of the Shepherd, carrying a sheep. It was as if in baptism, the Good Shepherd gathers up the sheep, one by one, forming them into one flock. It is now still as if the house of the church were the *aule*: there the voice of the crucified and living shepherd is heard in word and sacraments, and the people of God go in and out through the open door of his resurrection, finding life through Christ.

FIRST LESSON: ACTS 6:1-9; 7:2A, 51-60; 2:14, 36-41; 2:42-47; NEHEMIAH 9:6-15

The first reading precedes this Shepherd discourse with the account of the appointment of the Seven and the martyrdom of Stephen. Regardless of its historical background, this is an account much shaped to the purposes of Luke-Acts. Diversity of community and of ministry in the earliest church are harmonized into an ideal whole, with the Twelve appointing the Seven (6:6). The speech of Stephen (7:2-53) becomes a characteristic Lukan speech (cf. 13:16-41), reciting the history of law and prophets in order to proclaim Christ, the final action of the God of the outsiders. The whole continues to motivate the symbolic movement of the book from Jerusalem outward to the Gentiles: in this further act of rejection, made to parallel the Lukan passion of Christ, the murderers of Stephen lay their garments at the feet of Saul (7:58), who will become the great missionary of the Acts.

When read in the fifty days and at a celebration of the eucharist, we hear in this text the ministry of the word from one who was also called a server of tables (6:2-3). We hear that, in the midst of his persecution and death, he saw the very glory of God and the risen one, standing because he is risen, because he is coming to receive Stephen. We are invited to see in the word of God and the table of the church, now, that same vision, transforming the worst of fear and death into hope and forgiveness. Read next to the Gospel of the day, that vision of Stephen becomes an image of the open gate for the sheep.

The Roman Catholic lectionary appoints **Acts 2:14, 36-41** for this day, reading the conclusion and the result of Peter's sermon on the Day of Pentecost: thousands were baptized (see above, on the Third Sunday of Easter). Read next to the Gospel, this text may cause us to think of the Dura baptistry. The Shepherd gathers the sheep through the font.

The Revised Common Lectionary reads the description of the common life of the earliest community in **Acts 2:42-47** (see above, on the Second and Third Sundays of Easter). Here is the very *aule* of the Shepherd.

The Episcopal lectionary provides **Nehemiah 9:6-15** as the alternative that might be read from the Old Testament. This pericope includes the beginning of the great prayer of the Levites (or, of Ezra, according to the Septuagint), proclaimed at the rite of atonement that was celebrated in the early post-exilic Jerusalem. These gatherings for prayer and for the reading

of the Law reported in Nehemiah 8–9 have often been called "the Great
Synagogue" and seem to have exerted a considerable ongoing influence in
the formation of synagogue liturgy. The prayer of the Levites (9:5-37)
itself follows the pattern of thanksgiving and beseeching that came to mark
so clearly both Jewish and Christian prayer. The alternate pericope, however, includes only the great thanksgiving section of that prayer—and that
only up to and not including either the combination of that thanksgiving
with confession (9:16-31) or the beseeching (9:32-37). This editing means
that the text can stand as a summary of the great acts of God's merciful
deliverance, against which background the resurrection of the Shepherd is
to be proclaimed. God still delivers. Even now, "bread from heaven" and
"water out of the rock" of Christ (9:15) are set out to human hunger by the
God of the exodus and the return from exile.

PSALM 23

Psalm 23, the great shepherd psalm, may have originally been a royal
psalm: the king in Israel (who would have been called "shepherd" in the
religio-political idiom of Near Eastern peoples) asserting that the LORD is
shepherd of the king. But it has provided much wider comfort to generations and generations of Jewish and Christian believers with its splendid
images of comfort and refreshment. In Easter, Christians hear christological resonances in its verses: Jesus is the one whom God has brought
through the "valley of the shadow of death" (23:4). Sung "in Christ," on
this Sunday, it says even more to the assembly: The Shepherd is there for
Stephen, setting out a table to him who served tables. So also, the Shepherd is there for the people. See: in baptism, you come by the waters and
are anointed with oil. In the eucharist, your cup already overflows. The
God of ancient deliverances sets you free from fear.

SECOND LESSON: I PETER 2:19-25

The second reading provides the only time in the fifty days in which we
will read from 1 Peter out of order (we will skip back to the beginning of
the second chapter next Sunday). The reason for this choice is, of course,
the provision of the sheep/shepherd image in 2:25 as a parallel to the
Gospel text. The text itself is drawn from the "household code" of 1 Peter
2:11—3:12, a long exhortation to particular groups of people about their
duties, introduced with the general admonitions of 2:11-17. "Household
codes," a particular feature of deutero-Pauline literature (cf. Eph. 5:21—
6:9; Col. 3:18—4:1, and material in 1 Timothy and Titus), have evoked

much scholarly discussion. While unique in the New Testament to deutero-Pauline writings, they are not uniquely Christian. Do they serve the purpose of strengthening Christian ethics and thus Christian distinctiveness against the world? Or do they do the opposite? Are they intended to use conventional household behavior apologetically (see 1 Peter 2:12, 15), so that nonbelievers will praise and be drawn to the Christians? Are they evidence of the institutionalization of the churches—into *households*, indeed!—in the face of declining eschatological expectation?

Whatever the answer, our text is about the behavior of *slaves*. That makes this text part of the problematic New Testament attitude toward slavery, an attitude that ongoing Christian insight, drawing from deeper sources of New Testament thought, has had to correct. In our pericope, the correction comes by simply leaving out the introductory verse of address (2:18), making the counsel to ancient slave-workers counsel to us all. One may rightly ask whether this is correction enough. The acquiescence to beatings, even for doing wrong (2:23), is problematic for us. The counsel to patient endurance under injustice, while often immensely important, is not always right. It belongs more to the spirit of the Roman household than to the magnificent ancient Christian hymn it quotes as a way of Christianizing the otherwise conventional ethics of the code.

That hymn, the probable source of 2:22-25, would have been a Christian reworking of Isaiah 53, the so-called Fourth Servant Song. This hymn is the real center of the pericope when read on this Sunday. The Shepherd of the Gospel is, for Christians, the Servant of the ancient Isaian poem: He rules and "shepherds" by his death. The Lamb of Isaiah 53:7, amidst all of us straying sheep (53:6; 1 Peter 2:25), has become the Shepherd (and Bishop!). Believing this will have ethical consequences. The use of the hymn in a table of duties rightly shows that. But, while confessing this Lamb may bring us into suffering with him, like Stephen, it will not always bring us to endure in *silence*. Stephen did not!

One final point: While others in our midst have taken up the "shepherding" work, being called by these very names of "pastor" and "bishop," they need to pay attention to the very serious warnings to religious leaders in these texts. Let them not hurt and destroy. Jesus Christ, crucified and risen, is pastor and bishop. Let their ministry be full of his cross and his risen, gathering, nondominating voice.

LITURGICAL CONSIDERATIONS

The *liturgy* of the entire fifty days has yet another ecumenically shared characteristic: Its eucharistic prayers frequently laud Christ as the Lamb.

The most ancient preface (*praefatio*, "proclamation," that initial proclama-
tory praise of Western eucharistic prayers) for the Sundays of Easter
includes this line: "for he is the true Passover Lamb who gave himself to
take away our sin, who by his death has destroyed death, and by his rising
has brought us to eternal life." Such a phrase will stand out in our ears on
this Sunday. "True Lamb": there is that same Johannine tendency to
attribute so many images of life—true vine, bread from heaven, good
shepherd—to Jesus Christ. Only now, the striking thing is that the Lamb is
the Shepherd. In fact, the way he is the Lamb is exactly the same way he is
the Shepherd, and it can be seen in this meal: not by ruling, but by being
mortal lamb amidst wandering sheep and by giving himself away that all
may live.

Fifth Sunday of Easter

Lectionary	First Lesson	Psalm	Second Lesson	Gospel
Revised Common	Acts 7:55-60	Ps. 31:1-5, 15 16	I Pet. 2:2-10	John 14:1-14
Episcopal (BCP)	Acts 17:1-15 *or* Deut. 6:20-25	Ps. 66:1-11 *or* 66:1-8	I Pet. 2:1-10 *or* Acts 17:1-15	John 14:1-14
Roman Catholic	Acts 6:1-7	Ps. 33:1-2, 4-5, 18-19	I Pet. 2:4-9	John 14:1-12
Lutheran (LBW)	Acts 17:1-15	Ps. 33:1-11	I Pet. 2:4-10	John 14:1-12

The Fifth Sunday in the *pentecost* of Year A presents us with a rich depth of textual material. We not only read the important "many mansions"/"way, truth, life" pericope from the Fourth Gospel. We also encounter the "living stone"/"royal priesthood" text from 1 Peter and the marvelous phrase of Acts 17:6: "These people who have been turning the world upside down have come here also." All of these texts have been important to generations of Christian thinkers and preachers. In many ways, no commentary can exhaust them. But today we read the texts in the light of Easter, encountering the one who lives in the midst of them: The risen Christ comes again to take us into the way, truth, and life. The assembly around Christ who is present in word and sacrament drinks the milk of the word, tastes the goodness of the Lord, and is formed into the house of the Spirit. And the people of this Easter faith are called to continue to turn the whole inhabited world upside down.

On first glance, however, the Gospel text does not seem to have to do with Easter. It seems we have come to yet another case of the "wrong words" for speaking the resurrection (see above, on the Fourth Sunday of Easter). That is true, of course. We have no other words. But the Gospel readings for the Fifth, Sixth, and Seventh Sundays of Easter, in all three lectionary years, do bear a special relationship to Easter faith and to primitive accounts of the death and resurrection of Jesus. On these Sundays, the appointed texts are drawn from the great final discourse in the Fourth Gospel (John 13:31—17:26). We have already seen how the discourses in John often bear an important relationship to the "signs," with which they are interwoven and for which they may serve as the same revelation in the form of *words*. The final discourse is also related to a "sign." It is the greatest of the signs, the one toward which all the others have pointed: the death and resurrection of Christ.

The final discourse, then, is a collection of words for that death and resurrection. That is why the image of "going away" and "coming again" recurs so frequently (13:33, 36; 14:2-4, 12, 18-19, 23, 28; 16:5, 7, 10, 16-

22; 17:11, 13) as the principal "figure of speech" (*paroimia*; 16:25) in the
discourse: Where Jesus is going is *death*; his return is his *resurrection*.
Because of this structure of the Fourth Gospel, the Western church (and the
Eastern church, too, on the Seventh Sunday) has rightly turned to this great
"Farewell Discourse" as source for the words of Easter.

GOSPEL: JOHN 14:1-14

The Gospel for the Fifth Sunday stands at the beginning or near the beginning of the final discourse. It forms one of the major presentations of the
"going away" figure of speech, continuing a discussion that began at 13:33
(cf. 13:1, 3). The very metaphor of journey allows the Johannine Jesus to
assert, "I am the way . . ." (14:6). It is thus the crucified Jesus, the one who
"goes away," who is the way. But the way to what? While his "going
away" is his death, there is another sense in which that journey is to God,
toward being hidden in God. He is gone, not to be seen, unfollowable,
because he is dead, but also, says faith, because he has gone to God (13:33,
36; cf. Col. 3:3). Indeed, at the very hour in which his "departure to God"
(13:1) has arrived, what he does is the slave-service (13:4-5) that foreshadows the cross. The Fourth Gospel intends us to know that "going away" to
God is not the mythic processional journey of a spiritual potentate travel-
ing through light realms accompanied by angels. It is Jesus' awful death.

But, for the believing community, he comes again. He comes not, in
John, at the end of time, but now, in the resurrection. Then the possibility
of following the "way," of going to God, becomes available to the community. But Jesus is not just a guide, a revealer of the secrets that will get us
to God. He is himself the revelation of the goal of the journey. To see him
is to see the Father (14:9). He is the way; he is also the truth and the life.
His "I am" already suggests that, by being the very name of God. Indeed,
in John's Gospel, because these things are proclaimed in the community
after the resurrection, time itself is collapsed. For Thomas to see the risen
one was, at the same time, to see the crucified one in his wounds (20:26-
27), but in a new way; for him to see the one who went to God in death
(20:17) was to see "my Lord and my God" (20:28). So, for the community
to see the one who "comes again" in the resurrection is to see the one who
"goes away" in death. For it to see the one who has gone to God, is to see,
now, here, God! "Believe in God," says Jesus. "Believe also in me" (14:1;
cf. 14:11).

If Jesus is going to "my Father's house" (14:2), then, there is another
sense in which he himself, in his crucified and risen body, *is* "my Father's
house." He is the new temple (2:21-22; cf. 2:16), the true "place" (*topon*,

as 11:48 calls the temple), the very dwelling place of God (*ho pater en emoi menon*, 14:10), the locus of God's appearance and words and works. But then the dwelling places (*monai* and *topon*, 14:2) that Jesus prepares for the believing community are not features in a heavenly speculation about life after death. They are found in his cross, the place where he draws all (12:32). They are indeed where he is (14:3), and he is risen, in the midst of the community, drawing all to faith and life and God. This community, the very place represented by Thomas and Philip in the dialogue of the text, is now the locus of the "greater works" of drawing all the world to faith and hope, precisely because of Jesus' death (14:12). In doing so, the community will draw people into a genuine dwelling place, a home, where they may be with Jesus where he is, and so be with God.

Read in Easter, this text provides astounding words for the resurrection. With so many people remembering the use of this text from countless funerals and with the text itself full of images for Jesus' own death, the preacher will have occasion to speak of death, sorrow, hiddenness, and loss. But "I will come again and take you to myself" (14:3) is not a word, in the first place, for the end of the world or the end of one person's life. It is a word for the church, in assembly. It is the meaning of Easter, now. The proclamation of the resurrection is not an idea about life after death, nor even simply an idea about Jesus. It is, says faith, Jesus himself, who was crucified and seems absent, acting in the midst of our sorrow and death to gather all people into the life of God now. Because of the presence of this Jesus in word and sacrament and assembled body, this place is now "the house of God."

FIRST LESSON: ACTS 17:1-15; 6:1-7; 7:55-60; DEUTERONOMY 6:20-25

The first reading presents a part of the missionary journeys of Paul, this time to Thessalonica and Beroea, accompanied by the very Silas whom we have come to know as the "Silvanus" of 1 Peter 5:12. The two accounts are stylized presentations: arrival at the synagogues, teaching from the Scripture, conversions, opposition. The most interesting verse, perhaps drawn from an independent source about the sufferings of a certain Jason, is the accusation at 17:6. "World," in this case, is *oikoumene*, "the whole inhabited world." Read in Easter, the text follows the pattern of seeing the expansion of the church as the "acts of the risen Christ." Read next to the Gospel for the day, the text might help us see that the astounding idea that a crucified man is the dwelling place of God does indeed turn the world—certainly the religious and political world—upside down.

Both the Roman Catholic and the Revised Common Lectionaries read, instead of this account, differing portions of the story of Stephen, the Roman lectionary the appointment of the Seven (**Acts 6:1-7**) and the Revised Common Lectionary the vision of Stephen and his death (**Acts 7:55-60**). For a discussion of these texts in Easter, see above on the Fourth Sunday.

The Episcopal lectionary allows its usual alternate from the Hebrew Scriptures, in this case, **Deuteronomy 6:20-25**, which presents a question from children and a creedlike response which recites the mighty deeds of God. For the question-and-answer form one should compare material in the Passover observance (e.g., Exod. 12:26-27); for the response one might compare the famous text in the first fruit ritual (Deut. 26:5-10). In Deuteronomy, the text makes clear that, according to the point of view of that material, all the legal development in Israel needs to be seen as a witness and memorial to the exodus and the giving of the land. The law then is to be obeyed "to keep us alive" (6:24). For the Christian, for whom the equation between obedience and life will never be that simple, the Deuteronomy text must be subjected to a certain criticism, a criticism that is already present in the Hebrew canon (Job!) and that can be represented by the surprises of the Gospel text. Easter preachers should avoid preaching Deuteronomic orthodoxy in an unbroken fashion. But, in Easter, the list of the deeds of God for deliverance will continue to play an important role behind the proclamation of the resurrection. And the preacher will want to have something of the spirit of one who tells the children, in every generation, "We were slaves, but the Lord brought us out!"

PSALM 31; 33; 66

The Psalm is, once again, one of many. The Revised Common Lectionary appoints parts of **Psalm 31**, an individual lament, as if it were singing with Stephen: "Let your face shine upon your servant" (31:16), and "Into your hand I commit my spirit" (31:5). The Roman Catholics and the Lutherans sing fragments of **Psalm 33**, a hymn that echoes the upside-down world with "Sing to the LORD a new song" (33:3). For Easter use, the most important verse is probably 33:19 in which God's deliverance from death is celebrated. The Episcopalians sing the part of **Psalm 66** that is a communal thanksgiving, appropriately responding to the Deuteronomy text with yet more recitation of the "awesome deeds" of God. For Easter, the fragment ends in a way echoed by the faith in the resurrection of Christ that leads us all out to life: "We went through fire and water, but you brought us out to a place of refreshment" (66:11 in the *BCP* Psalter).

SECOND LESSON: I PETER 2:1-10

The second lesson is probably the most central and stunning passage in that deutero-Pauline letter. In reading it, one easily imagines the text as addressed to the newly baptized—as if they were standing dripping wet before us—and so to all the baptized. The opening verse sounds like a moral encouragement based on the remembered ritual act of stripping off old clothing before the immersion. The following passages can be heard as invitation for the "newborn" from the water to come to the assembly around the "milk of the word" (a better translation, here, than "spiritual milk") and the taste of the goodness of the Lord, indeed, to come into the community that is the very house or temple of God. The text makes use of traditions that interpreted Christ as the stone of Psalm 118:22 and the community as new Israel, a "people of priests and kings" (as Exodus 19:6 declares of the exodus slaves newly come to Sinai), a people who have now received mercy (as Hosea 2:1, 23 promises to repentant Israel). And the passage builds on the tradition that a God-built temple will replace the human-built religious shrine: the community, gathered around the crucified Christ, is both that building and its "priesthood."

Read in Easter, the text awakens us again to the presence of the newly baptized in our midst, calling us all to come afresh to the meaning of our baptism. This pericope, in fact, provided the antiphon of the *introit*—and thus the title—of the old Western Second Sunday of Easter: *Quasimodo geniti*, "As newborn babes, alleluia, desire the sincere milk of the word, alleluia." The antiphon recalled that baptisms had occurred at *pascha* and that the *pentecost* was now a time of mystagogy in word and sacraments.

Read next to today's Gospel , the "house" of this text is seen to echo the "house" of John 14. The world is full of people who are indeed exiles, "no people," "not pitied." This Easter house—a dwelling place prepared, the risen Christ taking each one to himself—is for them. So is the task of the "priesthood": declare the deeds of the one who brings them into light.

LITURGICAL CONSIDERATIONS

One might hold next to these texts this phenomenon from the Easter liturgy: Since earliest times, since Tertullian and then the council of Nicea, at least, people have come to communion during the fifty days, standing. This ancient practice may have fallen out of use in our times, but it is worth recovering. Raised up together with Christ, made to stand in baptismal dignity, the Christians of Easter hear these calls to movement and to action: "I am the way"; "Come to him, a living stone"; "Taste and see that the Lord is good." "These people who have turned the world upside down have come here also.

Sixth Sunday of Easter

Lectionary	First Lesson	Psalm	Second Lesson	Gospel
Revised Common	Acts 17:22-31	Ps. 66:8-20	I Pet. 3:13-22	John 14:15-21
Episcopal (BCP)	Acts 17:22-31 or Isa. 41:17-20	Psalm 148 or 148:7-14	I Pet. 3:8-18 or Acts 17:22-31	John 15:1-8
Roman Catholic	Acts 8:5-8, 14-17	Ps. 66:1-7, 16-20	I Pet. 3:15-18	John 14:15-21
Lutheran (LBW)	Acts 17:22-31	Ps. 66:1-6, 14-18	I Pet. 3:15-22	John 14:15-21

GOSPEL: JOHN 14:15-21; 15:1-8

The Gospel for this Sunday continues the pattern, established last Sunday, of speaking of Christ's death and resurrection as "going away" and "coming again." But by the kind of circular speech common in John's Gospel, in which the same themes are repeatedly revisited but also broadened and connected, this text deepens the understanding of both "departure" and "return." The death of Jesus begins here to be seen as the occasion of the gift of the Spirit of God to the community (14:16-17; cf. 16:7). And his return in the resurrection is seen as bringing both life (14:19) and access to the Father (14:20-21). Indeed, just beyond the end of our pericope, it is asserted that in the resurrection/return of Christ the believer becomes the dwelling place of Jesus and the Father. For us, on this Sunday, this text comes to invite us to see our liturgical assembly as drawn into the very presence and life of the holy Trinity because of the death and resurrection of Christ.

The Spirit will "abide" (*menei*) with the community (14:17). The Fourth Gospel asserts this, using the very verb that is also used of the abiding of the community in Jesus and the abiding of Jesus in them (15:4). This verb also hovers behind the noun, *mone*, "dwelling place," "home," which the Farewell Discourse uses of the place being prepared for believers in the Father's house (14:2) and for the presence of Jesus and the Father in the believer (14:23). The Spirit who so abides in the community is that Paraclete or Comforter or Advocate so often mentioned in the discourse (14:16, 26; 15:26; 16:7). The name need not divert us: this is that Spirit of God, God present and active, who will comfort and advocate by enlivening the remembrance of Jesus and of Jesus' words. The community around the remembrance of Jesus is alive to the universal significance of the events in Jesus—is capable of "greater works" than the historical Jesus (14:12)—precisely because Jesus has died and the Spirit has come.

Jesus has died and the Spirit has come. While the Spirit comes from *God* (14:16), is God present and active, in another sense, the Spirit is sent and given by Jesus, by the death of Jesus (16:7), or by the dying prayer of Jesus (14:16). This assertion has already been implied in John's Gospel, in the passage about water flowing from the heart (7:38-39). But that passage is made explicit in the passion account: from the heart of the *crucified* (that is, John's *glorified* one) there flows the water of the Spirit as well as the blood of death (19:34). Indeed, Jesus' dying breath is also a handing over of the Spirit (19:30). In case we have not gotten the point, the risen crucified Christ both shows his wounds and breathes out the Spirit (20:20, 22). Thus, the spirit active in the community is the very holy Spirit of God insofar as it bears witness to Jesus Christ. Moreover, Jesus' death is made larger, world redeeming, more than just one ancient sorrow about one ancient man, because God has given the Spirit through his death. Because of this gift, the world is proved wrong about sin, righteousness, and judgment (16:8-11)—in other words, about its very relationship with God—and not just about the evil judgment of one more innocent victim.

But if the Spirit enlivens the community because of Jesus' death, his resurrection has brought the very access to the Father. By his death, they were "orphaned" (14:18). In his resurrection, these orphans have a "Father" (14:20-21). This Johannine language for God—for God as the creator of the world and the source of Jesus—is dependent upon the common Hellenistic idiom for the "father of the gods" (Zeus Pater, Jupiter, Zeus the Father), upon ancient biology that saw only the father as source of the child, the mother being simply an "envelope" or a "flowerpot," and especially upon the biblical and synoptic tradition of speech about God. In the latter, God is the "father" especially of the king (cf. Ps. 2:7). When the Synoptic Jesus is then called the "son" or when he calls upon god as *"Abba,"* the tradition is making use of a complex symbol but it is primarily asserting that this Jesus is the Messiah of God, the new and eschatological "king."

John is asserting more. For the Fourth Gospel, this God is no Zeus, nor a Zeus-influenced Hebrew Scripture monarch. Rather, God is the source of Jesus. And seeing Jesus is seeing this "Father" (14:9). Indeed, when the community knows the risen one as abiding in its own midst, it is invited to know that all that God is—the creator and life giver and covenant maker—has come with Jesus risen and is accessible to the community.

This very Johannine use of the language should caution us from turning the word *Father* here into an excuse for a new Zeus-ifying of God. *Father* is a word from the biblical tradition and from the then-current culture. In the use of the Fourth Gospel, that word is transformed to say that the very God for whom both the tradition and the culture hope is the source of Jesus. Because of the resurrection, this God has also become the end of our loneliness and desolation, our "orphanhood." But all that we know of this God, we know in the serving, crucified Lord. Knowledge of God comes with knowledge of Jesus, not by speculation on God's sexuality or on God's monarchy or on God's omnipotence.

The promises of this text—promises of the abiding Spirit and of the life-giving return of Jesus—are spoken to the community, to a plural "you." But then, in a characteristic Johannine way, the final promise of revelation (14:21), foreshadowing the promise of "indwelling" (14:23), is spoken to an individual, to a singular type. One should be careful in interpreting this fact, however. These variations in number are rather like the narrative variations between Mary Magdalene or Thomas and the entire assembly in chapter 20. The Gospel of John has a "personal-communal" word, a message to the assembly that is also appropriated by individuals. But it does not have an individual mysticism. The Jesus who reveals himself to an individual in 14:21 is the same Jesus who is seen by the community in 14:19. In fact, the event of seeing or revelation here is the same event. The NRSV is right to translate 14:21, 23 with plurals. That is the more so, since the very "word" or commandment which the individual in 14:21, 23 is to keep is the commandment of communal love (13:34; 15:12).

But one should be careful in understanding the word keep (*terein*), the verb that frames this whole pericope. It does surely mean "observe" or "do" in the sense of any legal observance, but the word or "law" to be observed is the law of communal love. Such observance is not a matter of a simple checklist or a collection of "do's and don't's." It is life with the community for which Jesus died—and life according to that very measure of love (15:12). Even more, the words of Jesus are not just to be "done." They are to "abide" in the community (15:7), just as the Spirit (14:17) and the risen one himself (15:4) abide in the community. Indeed, the words themselves are active: They cleanse the community (15:3). This "keeping" is rather more like that of Mary in the Lukan infancy narrative (Luke 2:19, 51; *sunterein* and *diaterein*) who keeps all the "things" or "words" of the birth of Jesus, pondering them in her heart. But then the words of Jesus, the Spirit of God enlivening the words of Jesus (14:25-26), and even the very returned presence of the risen one and so of the Father—these all and these all *together—abide* in the community, forming it into the community of love.

Read in Easter, this text will be heard to center in 14:19 as a summary of the Easter Gospel: "In a little while the world will no longer see me, but you will see me; because I live, you also will live." Much of our Easter homiletic has been exploring how Jesus is "seen" in the "mysteries," in word and sacrament present in the assembly. But now we are invited to see that the life-giving, returning one comes with the very life of the Trinity. The cleansing, life-giving words, the enlivening Spirit, and the very access to God are all present in the community because of the death and resurrec-

tion of Christ. This Sunday is a kind of Trinity Sunday and Day of Pentecost, rolled together into one and already celebrated within the fifty days.

The lectionary of the *Book of Common Prayer*, proposing the pericope
we have been considering as a text for the fifty days in Year B, reads **John
15:1-8** on this Sunday in Year A instead. While this choice misses the trinitarian character of 14:15-21— and so the explicit chance to celebrate the
Trinity as heart of the mystery of the resurrection—it does enable three of
the Sundays of Easter to be focused on the "I AM" sayings of the Johannine Jesus. The Fourth Sunday had "I am the gate" (with "I am the Good
Shepherd" hovering behind it). The Fifth Sunday had "I am the way, the
truth and the life." And this Sunday has "I am the true vine." Such a series
gives a remarkable opportunity to explore both the depths of Johannine
theology and the depths of grace in the risen Christ.

The "vine" is, of course, an ancient metaphor for Israel itself (cf. Isa.
5:1-7), a metaphor that recurs in at least some of the lists of readings for
the great vigil of Easter. As such, "vine" or "vineyard" becomes a
metaphor both for the crucified and risen Christ and for the church that is
alive through him. Even more, "vine" is never far away from "tree," and
speculation concerning the tree-of-life or the world-tree may be behind
this pericope.

But John explores the metaphor. All that people hoped for in vines or
trees is found in Jesus risen. More, it is found in the paradoxical "I AM" of
Jesus: the crucified one makes use of the ancient divine name (Exod. 3:14;
cf. John 18:4-8), and in the crucified one as the presence of God are hidden
all the treasures of promise and grace and reality. John then uses this
metaphor to propose another approach to the very themes of mutual "abiding," of the word, and of access to the Father that we have already considered above. Read in Easter, this text of the vine gives yet another metaphor
for the death and resurrection of Christ and for the community which lives
from that death and resurrection. Now word and sacrament are a primary
means for the mutual abiding of vine and branches.

FIRST LESSON: ACTS 17:22-31; 8:5-8, 14-17; ISAIAH 41:17-20

The first reading is the account of Paul's famous missionary speech before
the Areopagus in Athens (**Acts 17:22-31**). This speech is, of course, another Lukan composition, representing an important view concerning the relationship of human religion and the proclamation of the gospel of Christ. In
that regard, it stands in some tension with the genuinely Pauline passage in
Romans 1:18-32.

In our series of readings from Acts, this passage represents the farthest expansion of the church's missionary circle. After the initial formation of the Jerusalem community around the word of the resurrection, we heard of Stephen and now we hear of Paul. What is more, we have now come to the place where preaching the one God must accompany the preaching of Jesus Christ: we have begun to see the development of the credal form of baptismal mission to the Gentiles.

The text does demonstrate to us one of the difficulties in reading Acts. The book is overwhelmingly focused on the men, largely ignoring the women, except as they are wealthy patrons of the community. This speech, for example, begins, in the Greek: "O men, Athenians . . . " (17:22). Such a form of address, widely echoed in the other speeches of Acts, is not accidental. While what follows may be immensely important for the church, it also must be read with an ear to the silence, to the life of the believing women of Christ who are not represented in this or in practically any other Acts text.

Read in Easter, the text from Acts may be used, nonetheless, to underscore the boundaries and limits in which we all live (17:26), especially the boundaries of our mortality and the limits of our knowledge. Read next to the Gospel, however, we are invited to see that we are not left to "grope for God" (17:27), hoping to transcend those boundaries, but that the risen Christ comes—and with him comes the full access to God—to us within those very boundaries.

The Roman Catholic lectionary proposes another reading from Acts, the account of the mission of Philip in Samaria (**Acts 8:5-8, 14-17**). The Roman series of first lessons, then, instead of expanding to the Pauline mission to the Gentiles, follows a nearer goal, expanding from Jerusalem and Judea to Samaria (cf. Acts 1:8). In both cases, however, an Easter trajectory that heads toward "the ends of the earth" is intended. That trajectory gathers up us and our present assembly, entraining us in the mission as well. The text itself presents some difficulties of interpretation. Rather than interest in the relationship of religion and Christian proclamation, this text seems motivated by the interest in church order: the apostles must come and confirm the work of Philip; the peripheral mission must be related to the center. If such a text is used to urge us to relate all mission to the "apostolic" word of witness to Christ and to a linkage of communities, it will be extremely helpful. If it is used to bolster hierarchical privilege and a rejection of those who have "only" been baptized in the name of Jesus (a practice elsewhere praised; cf. 19:5), then it must be used with great care. Uninterpreted, the idealizations of the church in Acts can still do considerable harm.

The Episcopal lectionary offers us again the strong alternative of a reading from the Hebrew Scriptures, in this case **Isaiah 41:17-20**. This passage, a song from Second Isaiah celebrating the return from exile as both a new exodus and a new creation, provides a rich imagery with which to celebrate the resurrection. Now the water provided to the thirsty is both the word of Christ and the promise that the earth itself will share in Christ's new life. Given the description of the trees that will grow in the wilderness (41:19), this text, when put next to the Episcopal use of the vine Gospel, can make of this Sunday a kind of Tree of Life Sunday in the church year.

PSALM 66; 148

The Psalm (**66**) in the Revised Common, Roman Catholic, and Lutheran lectionaries is the same psalm used in the Episcopal lectionary last week (see above). It is a combination of both communal and individual thanksgiving that may be seen to anticipate the combination of communal and personal encounter with Christ in the Gospel. The *Book of Common Prayer*, instead, continues the new creation and Tree of Life themes by using **Psalm 148**: "Praise the LORD from the earth . . . fruit trees and all cedars!" (148:7, 9).

SECOND LESSON: I PETER 3:13-22

The second reading is the passage that immediately follows the table of household duties in this Deutero-Pauline letter, and it probably demonstrates the principal reason for the inclusion of those duties. The writer seeks for the community to attract and not unnecessarily offend potential believers in Christ. The purpose of counsel on behavior is apologetic: "Always be ready to make your defense . . . for the hope that is in you" (3:15). Such defense, however, may bring suffering. But then Christ, whose death and defense before the ancient spirits of evil are recounted (3:18-20), is a model both for Christians and for the way of their baptismal survival amidst the evil and unlistening world. Since the baptismal way is the underlying theme of the letter, this passage forms, with the "new birth" of 1:3, an important bracket of the intervening material.

Read next to the Gospel of the day, this passage may prepare us to hear the Johannine version of the assertion about access to God through the presence of the crucified risen one: "Christ also suffered . . . in order to bring you to God" (3:18), says 1 Peter. Read in the *pentecost*, Christians will not help but see the eight survivors of the flood (3:20) as a prefiguring of the Eighth Day, the great eschatological day of survival, known both in our own baptismal life and in this feast of Easter (see Introduction).

LITURGICAL CONSIDERATIONS

The *liturgy* of these Easter days, surrounding these readings, may very well include a relatively frequent repetition of the greeting "Christ is risen!" with its response "He is risen indeed!" As well as being a ritual reminder of the faith of the community, this greeting may serve to show us the mutual love and mutual honor in which the community abides (Gospel), may express the word that abides in the community (Episcopal Gospel), and may be a tiny practice of the defense of hope that we are to speak in gentleness and reverence (second lesson). May the whole sermon on this day be such a greeting!

The Ascension of Our Lord

Lectionary	First Lesson	Psalm	Second Lesson	Gospel
Revised Common	Acts 1:1-11	Psalm 47 or 110	Eph. 1:15-23	Luke 24:44-53
Episcopal (BCP)	Acts 1:1-11 or Dan. 7:9-14	Psalm 47 or 110:1-5	Eph. 1:15-23 or Acts 1:1-11	Luke 24:49-53 or Mark 16:9-15, 19-20
Roman Catholic	Acts 1:1-11	Ps. 47:2-3, 6-9	Eph. 1:17-23	Matt. 28:16-20
Lutheran (LBW)	Acts 1:1-11	Psalm 110	Eph. 1:16-23	Luke 24:44-53

This festival is set in the celebration of the fifty days as a kind of Lukan island amidst an otherwise largely Johannine sea. This is so because the chronology of Acts 1 and 2 (especially 1:3 and 2:1), in which the appearances of the risen Lord take place during forty days and the descent of the Spirit occurs on the fiftieth day, has shaped the Christian festal calendar at the end of the Easter season. But it is also so because the Lukan accent on mission and on the universal rule of Christ, themes always present in these Sundays through the Acts readings, now comes to take center stage. This accent does not ultimately displace the strong Johannine exploration of the meaning of Jesus risen and of the presence of the holy Trinity in the assembly, matters that provide the principal focus of *mystagogy* in these fifty days. Rather, Ascension Day comes to balance the mysteries and to remind us that the risen Lord is present in all the world and that the gospel is for all the world.

There is also danger in Ascension Day, of course. That danger is present in the possibility that the whole idea of "ascension" will be conceived naively and therefore thought of as ludicrous and irrelevant according to contemporary knowledge of the cosmos. Or, even worse, the message of the texts will be read to signal Jesus' *absence*, not his universal presence. For the deepest correction of both of these misreadings, we have only to pay attention to what the texts of the day actually say. The assertions here are much more complex and much more helpful than is the continuing uncritical tradition of the three-tiered universe.

GOSPEL: LUKE 24:44-53; MATTHEW 28:16-20; MARK 16:9-15, 19-20

The Gospel for the day is the very end of the "first book" (Acts 1:1) of Luke. It itself provides an account of the "ascension," albeit one that differs slightly from that found in Acts 1. Nonetheless, this account together

55

with the beginning of Acts provides a kind of "hinge" for the entire two-volume work. Beginning in the temple (Luke 1:5-23), the Third Gospel has come again finally to the temple (24:53) as a place of praise and waiting. The community that has been formed around the words of Jesus (24:44)—words with which the now-concluding Gospel book is filled—and around the Scriptures (24:44-47) and the meal of Jesus (24:41-42), has now been made to be itself like old Simeon and Anna (cf. 2:25-38), a people of praise and expectation fulfilling the purpose of the temple. This community too, on the model of Anna (2:38), is to speak in witness. Only its witness is to extend to all the world. So, beginning from Jerusalem (24:47)—a city that had to be transformed by the word of the resurrection—the gospel that had its beginning in the first book is to be carried to the ends of the earth (Acts 1:8).

It is from this community that Jesus "withdraws" (Luke 24:51). While this parting involves being "carried up into heaven" (the most likely reading, on the principle of *lectio dificilior*, since the omission of the phrase was most likely done to harmonize the text with Acts 1), the meaning of that destination is not further specified and can be taken to indicate simply "went to God." What is more, this event seems to take place as part of the first communal encounter with the risen one, on "Easter day" itself. There are no forty days here. But the community of praise and expectation is not bereft. It has the words of Jesus and his own interpretation of the Scriptures: It has the Gospel book itself! It has the continued breaking of bread (24:35; Acts 2:42, 46). It has the very blessing of Jesus (Luke 24:50-51). It has the promise of the "clothing" and the power of the Spirit (24:49). And it has the task of mission stretching before it (24:47-48 and so all of Acts).

Read in Easter's fifty days and read in our assemblies, this text invites us to see our own communities formed in the doxological model of Simeon and Anna, at the beginning of Luke, and of the Jerusalem community at the end. We too have the child—or the broken bread—in our hands. We too have the Scriptures. The blessing of Jesus risen is for us. So is the promise of the Spirit. We have been exploring these mysteries in Easter. Now we are invited to lift our eyes to mission. But the mission itself is surprising, for the word to be spoken everywhere is *forgiveness* (24:47).

The Roman Catholic and Episcopal lectionaries propose alternate Gospel readings for this day. The Romans read the very end of Matthew (**Matthew 28:16-20**), not the end of Luke. This text carries many of the same themes we have seen in Luke—worshiping community, the teaching or "words" of Jesus, sacrament, mission—only now without the potentially problematic "withdrawal" of Jesus. Unlike Luke, Matthew ends with the promise of presence in the community and with no "ascension" at all. The

Episcopalians, on the other hand, allow **Mark 16:9-15, 19-20** as an alternative to the Lukan reading. This passage, of course, is part of one of the "conclusions" to Mark that are missing from the best ancient manuscripts. These conclusions represent ways that were found to deal with the astonishing but actual Markan ending in 16:8, an ending full of Mark's usual penchant for paradox and the cross. The conclusions themselves seem to be pastiches of such traditions and materials as we find in the other Gospels. In the case of the Episcopalian alternate reading, the materials are very largely Lukan, though with some vocabulary familiar from John ("signs") and Matthew ("Go into all the world"). One would do better to read the Third Gospel itself.

FIRST LESSON: ACTS 1:1-11; DANIEL 7:9-14

The first reading in all the lectionaries is the more familiar account of the "ascension." This text gives the core story—the "cult legend," if you will—for the day. Here are the forty days and the cloud and the missioning to the ends of the earth. But this text, too, bears closer reading. The forty days are, of course, symbolic. So is the cloud. Forty days were required for both Moses and Elijah to be prepared to see God and be witnesses to Israel (Exod. 24:18; 1 Kings 19:8). Forty days was the length of the flood, Noah and his family surviving to live before God (Genesis 8:6). In Jesus risen, the community has come through the flood, seen God, been sent as witnesses. And the cloud is the very witness of God's presence, like the cloud of the exodus (Exod. 13:21; 14:19), the cloud that brings the human being to the Ancient One (Dan. 7:13), or the cloud of the transfiguration (Luke 9:34-35). While the world sees Jesus as dead and gone—"withdrawn" in that sense—the faith of the community sees Jesus as *with God*. Jesus' meaning and presence therefore is universalized, is *everywhere*, as God is, and, at the same time, God's glory is accessible in Jesus. It is this which the community knows, not the calculations of times and seasons (Acts 1:7). This knowledge, when it is enlivened by the very Spirit of God, is quite enough.

Read next to the Gospel, these very differences from the earlier narrative—the forty days and the cloud—are then seen to be enriching interpretations of the community's faith. In order to make sense, the accounts do not require a three-tiered universe, nor an overly naive sense of "up" as the direction to God, nor a reliance on the symbolic dating as factual. Rather, the accounts are Lukan Easter proclamations. They are ways of proclaiming the meaning of the resurrection in alternate terms. The crucified Jesus, killed and gone in the world, dead with all the dead and lost ones, is found

L.S.? Milfg bur "up"

by faith to be the key to the Scriptures, the affirmation of God's eschatological promise of the Spirit for all flesh, the source of a universal mission
of forgiveness. He is found, indeed, to be present, continuing the work
which he has begun (1:1-2).

The Episcopal lectionary follows its usual Eastertide custom and also
appoints on this day an alternative first reading drawn from the Old Testament. It is **Daniel 7:9-14**, the part of the great first apocalyptic vision of
Daniel which reports the coming of the human figure ("son of man," in
older translations) to the Ancient One and the enthronement of that human
being in an indestructible kingship. This vision, preserved for us in Arama-
ic (which may have been its original language), was probably intended to
comfort those Jews suffering under the rule of Greeks in the mid-second
century B.C.E., asserting that the "beasts" of worldly empires were doomed
but that God was rather appointing human beings—the "holy ones of the
Most High" (7:18)—to rule. Read on Ascension Day, the text continues in
the Christian tradition of using the image of the enthroned human being,
the end of all beastly tyrannies, to interpret Jesus, his death and his resurrection. Then, read next to the Lukan texts, the pericope makes clear one
of the sources for the "cloud" and one way to understand where Jesus is
going: He is "enthroned," at God's behest, beyond and above everything
that is called "rule."

PSALM 47; 93; 110

Today's Psalm may be one of the so-called "enthronement psalms" (**Psalm
47; Psalm 93**), which oddly celebrate the LORD as king and ruler, with no
mention of any earthly dynasty, thereby potentially criticizing all other
rule and authority. Or it may be the royal psalm (**Psalm 110**) that has been
so strongly used in the Christian tradition to understand the Messiah-hood
of Jesus. In either case, the text means to receive the ascension tradition
and celebrate the faith that Jesus rules with the very rule of God.

SECOND LESSON: EPHESIANS 1:15-23

The second reading is the portion of the opening of this deutero-Pauline
letter where the thanksgiving that inaugurates the letter becomes the
beseeching prayer for its recipients. Here the prayer is for the community
to receive the Spirit that they might know the hope they have and the very
power of God. The nature of this power of God is then elaborated: It is the
power that raised up the crucified Jesus. It is the power that—to say the
resurrection in other terms—"enthroned" him with God's own authority

("at his right hand," 1:20), which is thus above all other authority, earthly or spiritual, and beyond all naming, even such mystical naming that may belong to "the age to come" (1:21). Such enthronement images are the application of the biblical tradition of kingship to the resurrection faith. But the tradition should not be taken literally. Indeed, the very idea *king* is utterly broken and transformed by being applied to the crucified Jesus. That is what the text means by saying that this Christ ("anointed king," thus) is "above" every rule and every name.

Read on Ascension Day, this text can become a prayer that the present assembly may have eyes enlightened by the very Spirit for which the writer of Ephesians prays. Indeed, the text may insert the assembly into the life of the Trinity: prayer to God for the gift of the Spirit to understand and live from the truth about Jesus, to be the very "body" of this head of all things. Read next to the Lukan ascension texts, the pericope may help us to speak the paradoxical character of the "rule" of Christt.

Seventh Sunday of Easter

Lectionary	First Lesson	Psalm	Second Lesson	Gospel
Revised Common	Acts 1:6-14	Ps. 68:1-10, 32-35	I Pet. 4:12-14; 5:6-11	John 17:1-11
Episcopal (BCP)	Acts 1:(1-7) 8-14 or Ezek. 39:21-29	Psalm 47 or 68:1-20	I Pet. 4:12-19 or Acts 1:(1-7) 8-14	John 17:1-11
Roman Catholic	Acts 1:12-14	Ps. 27:1, 4, 7-8	I Pet. 4:13-16	John 17:1-11a
Lutheran (LBW)	Acts 1:(1-7) 8-14	Psalm 47	I Pet. 4:12-17; 5:6-11	John 17:1-11

The last Sunday in the fifty days is actually *next* Sunday, the Day of Pentecost, the fiftieth day. On that day, the church celebrates the Spirit of God who takes all of the mysteries of Easter we have been considering and pours them into our hearts. This is the Spirit that enlivens our assembly so that its words and sacraments are indeed life-giving with the very life of God. This is that Spirit which is "our clothing," as Julian of Norwich says, "that for love wrappeth us and all becloseth us for tender love."

But the Spirit does not wait for next Sunday to come! There would be no church, no Sunday, no assembly, without the Spirit. All of the fifty days have been full of witness to the life-giving presence of God—the Holy Spirit, thus—which is poured out from the death and resurrection of Jesus and which enables the memory of that death and resurrection in our midst.

Still, the Spirit of God is free and sovereign. The Spirit of God is not a function of our organization and our appointment. So it is appropriate that, on this penultimate Sunday of the *pentecost*, we turn to patience and to prayer. God promises to answer this prayer for the Spirit, but it is right that we pray. Indeed, to pray before God for the life-giving Spirit is one form of what it is to be an assembly gathered in the name of Jesus Christ. These nine days between Ascension and Pentecost are the archetypical days of Christian prayer for the renewal of the face of the earth.

GOSPEL: JOHN 17:1-11

The Gospel for this Sunday is, then, not surprisingly, a prayer. Indeed, it is the first part of the great prayer of the Johannine Jesus with which the Farewell Discourse concludes. If the discourse has taken its primary metaphor of "going away" and "coming again" to be a way to speak of the death and resurrection of Jesus, this final passage turns that speech into prayer. Jesus is "coming to you, Holy Father" (17:11, 13), which is to say, he is about to die. These are words for his death. Yet he leaves behind the name and words of God (17:6, 8, 12-14, 17, 26), indeed, the very glory of God (17:22), and, therefore, the promise of his abiding and revealing presence (17:23, 26). These are words for the living encounter of the community with the crucified one. Jesus then prays that these gifts—the words, the name, the glory, the presence—will protect or "keep" the community, make it holy, gather it into God's own presence and give it real and visible unity (17:11, 15, 17, 21-23).

One word for this conception of the meaning of Jesus' death is glory. The "hour" of glorification (17:1; cf. 7:39; 12:16, 23-24; 13:1-5), like the "hour" of his "lifting up" (cf. 12:27-33; 3:14), is the time of his awful killing. But, in John's Gospel, that death is magisterial, the drawing center of all things (12:32), the presence of the "I AM" of God (18:4-6). To the world, Jesus is dead and gone. To the believing community, he is in God's glory (17:5), that is, in both the light and the weighty reality of God. That glory is now encounterable in the community (17:10, 22, 24; cf. 1:14). Indeed, unity in the community and the possibility of access to God both come through the presence of the glory of the crucified. Such is the meaning of "resurrection" in John.

But what has happened, in this prayer-form summary of the Farewell Discourse, to the "Advocate" or "Comforter?" The trinitarian faith of the Fourth Gospel is still quite in place. While the Spirit is not explicitly mentioned, the "name," words, glory, truth, knowledge, and "keeping" (17:1-12, 15) of Jesus and of the Father which are resident in the community are simply another way to speak about the presence of the Advocate in the community. For John, the Spirit enlivens the words of Jesus (14:26), makes clear the meaning of the going and coming of Jesus (16:7-11), declares the truth of Jesus which is the truth of the Father, the Source of Jesus (16:12-15). These enlivened words, this revealed truth, are present in John 17 and are the grounds of Jesus' prayer. In fact, the petition of this very prayer for the Christian community can be summarized so: "I will ask the Father, and he will give you another Advocate, to be with you forever" (14:16).

The God of this prayer, like the God of the whole Farewell Discourse, is no pyramid of hierarchical power. Rather, God is the profound presence of a unity of love (17:26), the source of the unity of the community itself. "Eternal life," life that is real and not illusory or death-filled, is present when the community knows this God (17:3).

At the end of the Sundays of Easter in Year A we read the beginning of this prayer. In Years B and C, on the same Sunday, the rest of the prayer is read. But in each of the years the pericope should be understood as *pars pro toto*: the text for the day is actually the whole prayer. The circular manner of Johannine speech—the very characteristic that sometimes makes

interpretation so maddeningly difficult in John—helps us here. While
17:1-11, our text, introduces the theme of "glorification" and begins to
pray for the actual community around Jesus at the time of his death (prayer
for all the hearers of the Gospel begins at 17:20), all the themes of the
prayer are begun here. The text is rightly read as a prayer for the church of
all times.

Read in Easter, this text gathers up all that has been proclaimed in these
days about the presence of the risen one in the mysteries of the assembly,
making that proclamation into a prayer. We beg God, by the Spirit, to continue to enliven the word and sacraments in our midst—the "name" of God
among us, the means whereby we meet the one who met Mary and Thomas
and the disciples going to Emmaus, the voice and presence of the Shepherd.
We beg God for the strength of these things among us, so that the church
may be one and all people be gathered into the knowledge of God and so
into life. We pray, thus, in Jesus Christ, to the Father, for the Spirit.

FIRST LESSON: ACTS 1:1-14; EZEKIEL 39:21-29

The first lesson begins the readings of the day, the readings that will ultimately bring us to this prayer of the Johannine Jesus, with an image of the
church at prayer. The different lectionaries include varying amounts of the
first lesson from Ascension Day (see above) in the pericope for today, but
all of them conclude with the first Lukan summary of the life of the earliest
Christian community, which prayed and lived "in one accord" (1:14; cf.
2:46; 4:24; 5:12). This summary has the community together in the upper
room, the place of their assembly (the same room of the Last Supper, Luke
22:12? Or a room like the one that will be used for the Sunday eucharist at
Troas, Acts 20:8? Or both?), and it names the Eleven and Mary, while
mentioning other men and women. The intention here is to create an image
of the church waiting at the still center, the hinge, of the Luke-Acts work,
receiving the Gospel-beginning (1:1), praying, and waiting for empower-
ing for the Acts-mission. Perhaps the mention of "sabbath" (1:12) is not
only an accidental description of distance. The mention of the Mount of
Olives, the mountain of God's eschatological coming (Zech. 14:4), certainly is not accidental. The community is living in the midst of God's
promised coming.

Read in Easter and next to the Gospel, this text invites our present
assembly to see its own gathering as a place of prayer, a sabbath rest, an
openness to the Spirit in the midst of God's eschatological acting. It proposes that this assembly, by its prayer and its use of word and broken bread,
should hold itself in continuity with the apostles, with Mary and other fig-

ures from the actual history of Jesus, and with all the assemblies of Christians. The Gospel reading will then give more content to the actual prayer.

The Episcopal lectionary has its usual Easter alternative, in this case a reading from Ezekiel (**Ezek. 39:21-29**). This passage is the summary at the end of a series of promises concerning the return from exile (Ezekiel 33–39), just before the description of the "new temple" (40–48) begins. Here, too, the imagery is a magnificent promise about the end of captivity and the availability of the unhidden face of God. Read on this Sunday in Easter, the Christian community hears the pericope promise the pouring out of the Spirit (39:29) on a new assembly of the set-free, on those gathered in the name of Christ, those who find God's face revealed in the resurrection of Christ.

PSALM 47; 27; 68

The Psalm for the day is either **Psalm 47**, the enthronement psalm used by some lectionaries on Ascension Day (see above), or **Psalm 27**, the beautiful individual lament that can continue the theme of the Spirit as the face of God, or **Psalm 68**, the obscure and difficult song (some scholars think it may be simply a collection of first lines of other, lost psalms—a table of contents, thus!) that, nonetheless, has some remarkable lines. Using this latter, Christians will hear the "wings of the dove" (68:13) and perhaps even the "snow" (68:14) as referring to the Spirit. In any case, 68:5-6 is not obscure: The God of the resurrection is none other than the God who acts for the poor.

SECOND LESSON: I PETER 4:12-19; 5:6-11

Our Eastertide *lectio continua* of 1 Peter comes to an appropriate ending in this Sunday's text, with its reference to the "spirit of glory, which is the Spirit of God" (4:14). But its most remarkable gift to us, at the end of the *pentecost*, is the reminder of suffering and the call to patience. The whole of 1 Peter has been about the shape of the baptismal life. Here that shape participates in the very death and resurrection of Christ, the pattern of suffering and of comfort. This shape is as true of this deutero-Pauline text, then, as it is of Romans 6:1-4. Read in Easter, the pericope helps us see that the resurrection life is often still experienced as promise, not as presence. Some other time, not now, the God of glory and grace "will restore, support, strengthen, and establish you." The very fact of that *promise* makes room in the text for the many, many people who are not yet so restored, for whom such support sounds far away and agonizingly desired.

But read next to the Gospel of the day, the references to "glory" stand out. Glory does indeed belong to the God of the end, the God of promise (4:13; 5:1, 4, 10). But the community knows that even now, as people share in the sufferings of Christ, the Spirit of glory, the presence of the knowledge of the unveiled face of God, rests upon them. That Spirit enables patience, and prayer, and life.

LITURGICAL CONSIDERATIONS

The "alleluia" of Eastertide *liturgy* will continue to sound right through next Sunday's celebration, applying the ancient Hebrew acclamation to the Christian assembly's greeting of the risen Christ. Indeed, "alleluia" will continue to be sung, in a more modest way, on *every* Sunday, especially around the reading of the Gospel, as a kind of memory of Easter and a salutation to the risen Christ, the key to all texts. But today, "alleluia" begins to be combined with *"veni,"* with prayer for the coming of the Spirit. It is right. We proclaim the resurrection and the presence of the mercy of God. We also wait. We wait, indeed, with Christ who prays. Both the proclamation and the waiting insert us into the trinitarian life of the true God. Word about that God is our mission to the world. Knowledge of that God is life itself.